THE HEART OF THE FATHER

THE HEART OF THE FATHER

366 INSPIRING DEVOTIONS
TO STRENGTHEN YOUR FAITH

PO Box 1599, Vereeniging, 1930, RSA

First LuxLeather edition 2016

Cover designed by Christian Art Publishers

Images used under license from Shutterstock.com

Set in 11 on 15 pt Palatino LT Std
by Christian Art Publishers

Printed in China

ISBN 978-1-4321-1580-7

16 17 18 19 20 21 22 23 24 25 – 10 9 8 7 6 5 4 3 2 1

Keep yourselves in God's love as
you wait for the mercy of our Lord Jesus Christ
to bring you to eternal life.

Jude 21

JANUARY

Love the Lord Your God

"Love the Lord your God with all your heart and with all your soul and with all your mind and with all your strength. The second is this: 'Love your neighbor as yourself.' There is no commandment greater than these." Mark 12:30-31

Mark 12 gives us a very clear command, and that is to love God with all your heart, soul, mind and strength, and your neighbor as yourself. You are part of the heart of God, our loving Father, and He meets you right where you are. The question is simple: How do you see God and how do you view yourself? Do you see God as loving and available? Do you see God as being involved in your life? Do you see Him as a loving Father in your life? How do you see yourself, as a child of God?

Know God is available and wants to have a relationship with you. Herein lies your knowledge of God and the way you can become one with Him. It is possible to know Him, His will and His voice. He is present, in your life and in everything you do. Together, you and God do have a relationship.

Live like Jesus

Be devoted to one another in love. Honor one another above yourselves. Never be lacking in zeal, but keep your spiritual fervor, serving the Lord. Be joyful in hope, patient in affliction, faithful in prayer. Romans 12:10-12

God wants us to be there for one another. He can work in you to grow and change you to resemble His character. Our purpose as humans is not only to be like Jesus, but to live in such a way that others can see Him through us.

How would Jesus have acted at your workplace? How would He have handled the problems you face? We must change into His character, and grow in our own lives.

We must love God with all our strength. God is our King. He asks us to offer our resources to Him – our gifts, time and steps towards godly living – and to live like Jesus. We are not to regard ourselves as more important, bigger and with a higher status. Rather, we must be humble. We are to be servants of each other, and serve others with our time, money and resources.

God Is Omnipresent

The LORD Almighty is with us. Psalm 46:7

This is one of the things that we generally battle to fully grasp: God is omniscient, omnipotent, omnipresent. He can do anything. He has everything under His control. He knows what is going on in this world and He knows what tomorrow will bring. He holds the whole world in His hands. He has seen the end, and He was there in the beginning. Still, there are people who wonder about things like sickness, pain, sadness, misfortune and violence in the world. They want to know where God is amidst these terrible things.

God has given us the gift of free will to make decisions, and therefore He allows us to decide for ourselves. But we so often make the wrong choice, and must bear the unpleasant consequences. However, we can never say that God has left us. He is God, and He will always be in control. He remains loving and is always available when we need advice. And that is the point: He is not "gone" or uninvolved; it is we who must make time more often to sit at His feet and listen to His voice.

We Are God's Children

We know that in all things God works for the good of those who love Him, who have been called according to His purpose. Romans 8:28

Do you realize the full extent of what that means? *In all things God works for the good of those who love Him*. This is how He works with His children.

Despite all the brokenness and heartache in this world, God *is* in control. Accordingly, we don't need to worry about anything. He will let everything work out for good. We also find this assurance in Psalm 138:8 where we read that God will ensure that things work out for the best, because there is no end to His love. I say it again: The Lord will fulfill His purpose for me, because His faithful love never ends.

The Lord will not abandon the work of His hands. Even after the worst thing you've ever done, the worst sin or incident in your life, you can still be sure that God will fulfill His purpose for you – all is not lost. He will never forsake you. Turn back to Him and know that His goodness knows no end.

God Is Still in Control

LORD Almighty, blessed is the one
who trusts in You. Psalm 84:12

God is in control of your life, and He knows what He is doing. He knows your work environment and your circumstances. He knows your feelings and emotions. He knows everything about you.

Think about the effect of throwing pebbles into a lake. When you throw a handful into the water, they make circles that flow into each other. It is the same with life. Every little thing we do has consequences. Not just in my life, but also in the lives of others.

Think about it this way: Every day thousands of pebbles are thrown into the water, and despite what we do and how rough the water seems, God is in control. He looks at our lives and He says that He will fulfill His perfect will and purpose for our lives. God cannot be limited by the choices we make.

Rejoice and Be Glad

Rejoice in the Lord always. I will say it again: Rejoice!
Philippians 4:4

Joyfulness must be part of our daily lives. It is wrong to think that Christians should always be serious and never smile.

Knowing that we are loved by God and on our way to heaven puts a song in our heart, a smile on our face and spring in our step every day.

The psalmist sums it up so beautifully when he says, "The Lord is my strength and my shield; my heart trusts in Him, and He helps me. My heart leaps for joy, and with my song I praise Him" (Psalm 28:7).

Today, be someone who radiates Christian joy. Light up another person's day with your laughter and joy, and in so doing, draw them a little closer to Jesus.

Relax, God Is in Control

In Him all things were created: things in heaven and on earth, visible and invisible, whether thrones or powers or rulers or authorities; all things have been created through Him and for Him. Colossians 1:16

Read and reread the above Scripture verse. Yes, God created all things in heaven and on earth, the visible and the invisible. He created thrones and powers, rulers and authorities. All things were created through Him and for Him. From the beginning He held the world in His mighty hand.

Why would you then lie awake at night and worry about all sorts of things? Have you forgotten that God is in control? You can take everything to Him and lay it down at His feet. The One who created heaven and earth will not leave you – His child – to your own devices! He will always care for you – even if it is sometimes in ways you don't understand. Remember not to become so comfortable in your life that you forget to ask the Lord to care for you, or to lend a helping hand to someone in need.

There in the Tough Times

"God has made me forget all my trouble and all my father's household." Genesis 41:51

These are Joseph's words after the birth of his eldest son. If there is anyone in history who should be allowed to complain, it is definitely Joseph. First sold by his own brothers as a slave, then thrown in jail for how many years, even though he was innocent. During this time he could easily have asked where God was. But as time goes by, we see how God reveals His perfect plan. From a jail bird, Joseph goes on to rule the land. We can see how God first put everything in place in order to care for His people – even if it only became evident years later.

Maybe it is a good idea to think about Joseph's life when we want to complain and ask where God is, when we think that He doesn't care. In those times when we think it's not going well with us, think about Joseph. And remember that you are also part of God's Master Plan. Maybe He is busy getting you into position to play your perfect and important role.

God Is Greater Than Our Plans

"You intended to harm me, but God intended it for good to accomplish what is now being done, the saving of many lives." Genesis 50:20

Joseph realized that many people survived because God allowed him to be sold as a slave by his brothers years before. He could see that people wanted to punish him, but that God had a critical and important plan for his life.

It is often easier to read about Joseph and understand God's plans than it is to see God's goodness in your own life. And it is very difficult to see that God has something better in store for you and to keep believing in the midst of a gloomy situation. He is in fact preparing you for something greater and needs to chisel away at you a little bit more. But what more can be said than this: God will never forget about you. Look beyond people's cruelty and rudeness, and see God. See His bigger plan for your life and rejoice, because like Joseph you will also say one day, "You intended to harm me, but God intended it for good"!

Learn from Mistakes

Jesus said, "Simon, Simon, Satan has asked to sift all of you as wheat." Luke 22:31

If you think you've had a bad day, think about how it would feel if Jesus were to tell you, "You will deny that you know Me." Can you imagine how Peter must have felt! What would you have done had Jesus told you, "I know that when you get to work tomorrow morning, you will deny that you know Me"? Would you also strongly disagree and try to convince Jesus of your loyalty and love for Him?

And what do you then do the following day? Exactly what Jesus said you would. And then you immediately want to know why He allowed it to happen if He knew it was coming! But that's not how Jesus operates – He allows you to make mistakes, because our mistakes are part of who we are, and they help us grow as Christians. It is not always easy or pleasant. It is awful to know that you have betrayed the Lord, but remember that it can be an opportunity to learn and grow.

Getting Up Again

Jesus said, "I tell you that you are Peter, and on this rock I will build My church, and the gates of Hades will not overcome it." Matthew 16:18

Who of us has never betrayed the Lord? Peter must have wished that this story never ended up in the Bible; after all, it's not something one wants to be remembered for. But much like our own mistakes and faults, they form part of our life story. They determine in a way who we are and where our growth lies.

Jesus – who knows everything, including the future – told Peter that he is the rock on which He would build His church. Jesus said this to Peter while knowing full well what he was going to do. He knew Peter was going to deny Him, but He also knew the extent of His grace and mercy.

So, when you stumble in your faith, get up, dust yourself off and ask for forgiveness. And remember: Jesus forgave Peter, and He will forgive you too if you humbly come before Him.

Who Is God to You?

> That which was from the beginning, which we have heard, which we have seen with our eyes, which we have looked at and our hands have touched – this we proclaim concerning the Word of life. 1 John 1:1

How do you see God today? What does He look like to you? How do you talk about Him? How do you think about Him? What is your opinion of Him? And of course, what is your opinion of yourself? Where do you see yourself in your relationship with the Lord? John says, "I saw Him. I touched Him. I listened to Him. I walked with Him." Jesus has been with the Father since the beginning; He is part of the Trinity. He became Eternal Life and made His dwelling with us.

I don't know about you, but this is very exciting! Here we have someone who was there, who touched Jesus, sat beside Him, accompanied Him to the Garden of Gethsemane, who was there when He rose from the dead, and who touched Him before the Ascension. That person said he would tell us about Him. Isn't that wonderful?

The Only Light

Every good and perfect gift is from above, coming down from the Father of the heavenly lights, who does not change like shifting shadows. James 1:17

James was a half-brother of Jesus Christ by birth and grew up with Him. James was the younger brother and looked up to Jesus. What James wrote must surely stem from his experiences with Jesus. He experienced the Light of God firsthand.

The devil wants to convince us that we can't trust this Light – just look at the world around you! He doesn't want us to entrust our lives to this Light. He wants us to doubt God, but we know that the evil one can't stand the Light.

We can't function without this Light in our lives. We must take control of our emotions and resist the devil. We must trust God whole-heartedly and surrender our lives to Him. How is it possible to want anything else? From James we get a wonderful testimonial of this Light.

Stop the Doubt

> The serpent was more crafty than any of the wild animals the Lord God had made. He said to the woman, "Did God really say, 'You must not eat from any tree in the garden'?" Genesis 3:1

In a way the devil still asks us this same question today. Did God really say you shouldn't do that? Will God really take care of you? Is He really with you? Would it really be so bad if you gave in this one time? And before we know it, we are caught between doubt and disbelief.

This is exactly what the devil wants. He puts doubt in our minds, and then he quietly sits back and watches us water the doubt and make it grow. In this way we drift farther from God. As children of God we ought to know better. We must actively resist the devil and, like Jesus in the desert, we must reprimand the devil over and over again with answers from Scripture. Know that the devil will tempt you, but ask – every day – for strength from above to decisively resist. You *can*, because you are a child of God.

Scary Shadows

What, then, shall we say in response
to these things? If God is for us,
who can be against us? Romans 8:31

Sometimes it is so easy to lose sight of the Light, especially when the media constantly tells us about the terrible state of the world, and that God is not in control anymore. Then we focus too much on our fears and get frightened by our own shadow. We know we shouldn't do it, but still we do.

The solution is simple: Look only to the Light. The closer you move toward the Light, the farther you are from the shadow. That is what Romans 8:31 tells us: God is on our side, so who can stand against us? Our earthly fears are nothing to God: He is in control of all creation. He is always there for us. He loves us and He is the answer to all our fears.

When you are blinded by your fears, think about today's verse. Remember how much God loves you, and that He will always be with you and protect you.

Who Am I?

This is what the LORD says – He who created you, Jacob, He who formed you, Israel: "Do not fear, for I have redeemed you; I have summoned you by name; you are Mine." Isaiah 43:1

It sometimes happens that when children go through a rebellious phase, they see a psychologist to discover themselves again. That's what we're going to do today – find out who we are. Or more precisely, who we are in God.

How you view yourself has a significant influence on how you see God and your relationship with Him. The way you live, how you witness to others about Him, and how you see and experience life, it all starts with your identity. And we know where our identity lies: We are children of God. He is our Father. We love because He first loved us. We care for others because He cares for us. And we don't have to be afraid of the world, because He takes care of us. We are precious and special and we have an important purpose to fulfill in this life.

Say to yourself: I am important and precious, because I am a child of the Most High God.

Alone Time

"Do not fear, for I am with you; do not be dismayed, for I am your God. I will strengthen you and help you; I will uphold you with My righteous right hand." Isaiah 41:10

At times we feel alone on our journey through life. Take note of the word *feel*. I say *feel* because we are in fact never alone. God is always with us. God has a plan for your life, though of course His plans for each of His children differ. Perhaps it feels like other people's lives are so much easier than yours. Maybe it feels as if no one else could feel so alone, and that their sacrifices are much smaller than yours. When you get stuck in this spiral, you get sucked in very fast and very deep, until it feels as if you're all alone on this earth.

We've all been there, but it is unnecessary to feel this way. God is here with us – as close as no other human could possibly be. We are never alone. God doesn't lie to us in the Bible. If He tells us that He is with us, then He is. We must just reach out in faith, and He will take our hand.

Wonderful Love

His love endures forever. Psalm 136

Our great God wants to show you His love. Sometimes people think that God is too strict. Since He is holy, He won't allow us to do anything enjoyable. And then they choose to turn down the offer. They say no thank you to God's love, just because they think they'll have to give up too much. People think life will no longer be fun. Our image of God, and how He wants us to see Him, is completely distorted by the world.

Have you made the decision to allow God's love into your life? If you've said yes to His love you will know that a life in His love is the best thing on earth. A life with Him is filled with joy and all the good things that the God of the Universe has in store for you. Say yes to God today and experience how wonderful it is to have your identity in Him.

The Palms of His Hands

"Can a mother forget the baby at her breast and have no compassion on the child she has borne? Though she may forget, I will not forget you! See, I have engraved you on the palms of My hands; your walls are ever before Me." Isaiah 49:15-16

Earthly parents know how intense their love for their children is. It really is something you can only fully grasp once you have your own children. It is a bond that is never broken. It may be morning, noon, evening; sickness in the middle of the night … you can't just say, "Sorry, I'm too tired, let's talk about it tomorrow." No, your whole life is dedicated to your children. It is absolutely impossible to forget them.

I sometimes think that we don't fully grasp the concept. We so often wonder if the Lord still cares about what we're going through. We think that He doesn't know how we feel. But He is right beside us. He is here. He will never forget you. He knows about your stress, pain, what you worry about. It is impossible for Him not to care for you or forget you. He loves you with an everlasting love.

Before You Were Born

"Before I formed you in the womb
I knew you, before you were born
I set you apart; I appointed you as
a prophet to the nations." Jeremiah 1:5

Before you were born, God knew you. Before He formed you, He had a plan for your life. When you read this Scripture verse it is impossible to believe that your life has no meaning. God has always known what your purpose in this life will be.

The problem is that sometimes we have all sorts of excuses for not following the path the Lord has for us and not doing the work He set out for us. You think you know yourself better than the Lord does. Yes, you know yourself well, definitely better than your friends, colleagues or spouse, but the Lord knows you inside out. He knows what's best for you.

We must stop making excuses for not following His plan for our lives. All we need to say is: "Here I am, Lord, use me." Then we'll experience His miraculous power in our lives.

Through the Waters

"When you pass through the waters, I will be with you; and when you pass through the rivers, they will not sweep over you." Isaiah 43:2

That is how the Lord feels about me. He made me, and no matter what happens He will protect me. We all have to pass through a river at some point. Think about this for a moment. From time to time our country is plagued by heavy rains and severe floods. Think about how many people get swept away by water that isn't even deep. We have great awe for the power of water.

But wait a minute. What about the Creator of the water? Will the One who created everything, yes, even storm water, not be able to protect you?

Remember – this is a metaphor – I'm not telling you to swim in a river in flood. See it as a representation of your life. God won't let you drown in the demands of life. He will save you; just stretch out your hand and let Him take hold of it.

Walking through Fire

"When you walk through the fire, you will not be burned; the flames will not set you ablaze." Isaiah 43:2

What is worse than water? Well, the answer is fire of course. Fire destroys, and there are few things that can stop it. Fire causes chaos and destroys everything in its path. What does the Lord say? When you have to walk through fire, the flames will not set you ablaze.

Wow. Everyone has at one time or another accidentally stepped on a burning coal. It is very painful and few people would be able to handle anything worse than that. Now we read about walking through flames, but not being burnt. Like Shadrach, Meshach and Abednego, we will also be able to walk through flames unharmed.

So, when you again find yourself in the proverbial fire of life, look around carefully. Stop being afraid and look with eyes of faith. You might just see the Lord Himself with you in the flames, protecting you.

My Heavenly Father

See what great love the Father has lavished on us, that we should be called children of God! And that is what we are! The reason the world does not know us is that it did not know Him. 1 John 3:1

In my own life the most wonderful title I can think of is when God calls me His child. When I hear in my quiet time, "You're not a preacher, you're not a pastor, you're not the guy from TV, you're not a writer, you're none of those things. You're My son, the one that I love. My beloved. The one I long to have a relationship with. The one I want to sit and talk with, and rule and work together with forever in heaven."

When I hear this, I receive renewed energy to do and run and work. The most wonderful assurance in this world is surely knowing that the God of the Universe is your Father.

You are His child, because He made you His child. God calls us His own children. Sometimes this is almost too great to fully understand.

Child of God

The Spirit Himself testifies with our spirit that we are God's children. Romans 8:16

Do you love something or someone more than your children? Think carefully. Do you love someone or something more? For me the greatest love there is, is the love between a parent and a child.

This entails giving up your life and making sacrifices morning, noon and night. You are willing to do or give anything for these little children in your life. This is the most ultimate love you can think of. You'll give your life for your children, work yourself to death, protect them, fight for them and do anything for them.

God says there is an even greater love than this, and that's the love He has for you. He loves you even more. Let me tell you, when I hear this in my quiet time, it bowls me over. How can He love me more than this? He tells you to come to Him and wills you to be His child. Then you'll experience love in a way you never thought possible.

Grow in Faith

Be diligent in these matters; give yourself wholly to them, so that everyone may see your progress. 1 Timothy 4:15

Paul told Timothy that his spiritual growth should be evident to everyone he comes into contact with. In other words: Can people who've known you for a long time see that there is growth in your life? Can people see how your vocabulary has improved, your temper, your patience, your love for your fellow man? Do you look more like Jesus?

What does your spiritual growth look like? Does it feel at times that you don't grow at all, or that you're worse off than when you started?

Remember, spiritual growth is not necessarily only to do with knowledge. Spiritual growth is not always about how often you attend church and what others say and think about you.

Spiritual growth is about one thing: Do you look like Jesus? Look at your life and be honest. Do you act like Jesus, and can people see His presence in your life?

Spiritual Fitness

Have nothing to do with godless myths and old wives' tales; rather, train yourself to be godly. 1 Timothy 4:7

Paul tells Timothy not to waste time on myths and old wives' tales. Rather, a person should use their time and energy to get spiritually fit. It takes time and energy to do so.

What do spiritually fit people look like? What do their vocabulary, deeds and thoughts look like? Physical exercise is important, but spiritual exercise is much more vital because it holds a promise of a reward, in this life as well as in the next.

Spiritual fitness is therefore not only for heaven one day. It holds a promise for you now. Something in your life, in your work, in your marriage, in your finances … anything can change if you get spiritually fit. The rewards are for now – if you become spiritually fit, your life on earth will get so much better.

Light in the Darkness

God, who said, "Let light shine out of darkness," made His light shine in our hearts to give us the light of the knowledge of God's glory displayed in the face of Christ. 2 Corinthians 4:6

You can only get spiritually fit and sharp if you practice. It doesn't happen automatically. The Scriptures tell us that light must shine out of darkness. Likewise He has also made His light shine in our hearts to give us the light of the knowledge of God's glory that is revealed in the face of Christ.

In the space you create to reach God, He shines a light to make things more clear and to make Jesus' glory evident. If you don't do this, no matter how old you are, there will be a downward spiral of darkness and decay inside you. Only God can illuminate your heart. You must create the space and time and add spiritual exercise to your daily routine, so that God can talk to you, and let His light shine in and through you. If this isn't the case, you're not growing and there is no spiritual advancement in your life.

Milk or Solid Food

Though by this time you ought to be teachers, you need someone to teach you the elementary truths of God's Word all over again. You need milk, not solid food! Hebrews 5:12

Spiritual exercise requires practice and time. It takes time to pray, read spiritual books, fast and attend church and small group meetings. Did Paul say that it was going to be easy? No, he said that we would toil and sweat. It doesn't happen by itself. It takes effort.

My wife ran the Two Oceans Marathon. And let me tell you, she trained hard. For someone who doesn't know, it would look like she just gets up and goes running without any effort. I'm actually the one who does it effortlessly. I keep up easily. I don't need exercise, because I drive my car alongside her while she jogs. It's easier that way, but I don't get any fitter. This is precisely how spiritual fitness works. It takes discipline and practice – otherwise you don't grow at all. Isn't it time for you to also get out of the car?

When You Pray

Pray continually. 1 Thessalonians 5:17

Sometimes we think it doesn't matter how often we pray, as long as we talk to God, even if it is only a quick prayer every now and then. Then we think that we're OK in our relationship with Him.

But this is one of the biggest mistakes we can make. I'm not saying that a quick prayer here and there is wrong, but it is certainly not the intimate relationship that God wants with us. One cannot have an intimate relationship with someone you only talk to now and then when you need an urgent favor.

We have the opportunity of having a close and loving relationship with our Father. And what is more, this is also what He wants. If we've experienced how it feels to be in the Father's presence, we wouldn't want it any other way. Then we will, without effort, be in constant prayer with the Father.

The Person in the Mirror

Anyone who listens to the Word but does not do what it says is like someone who looks at his face in a mirror and, after looking at himself, goes away and immediately forgets what he looks like. James 1:23-24

As we know by now, spiritual exercise requires time and effort. It doesn't matter where you are on your spiritual journey, you simply must practice. Get started and read your Bible today – it will gradually grow from, for example, one day a week to every day of the week. Then you can start to deepen your Bible study and even join a Bible study group.

You don't want to be someone who looks in a mirror and immediately forgets what you look like. That's what it is to be spiritually shallow. You see something – like yourself – without realizing its value.

One cannot have a proper relationship with God without knowing Him. And the only way to get to know Him is by reading His Word. Discover the treasure trove of what the Bible has to offer.

Tuned in to the Son

Jesus said to them, "Very truly I tell you, unless you eat the flesh of the Son of Man and drink His blood, you have no life in you." John 6:53

With the word *flesh* Jesus implies the Word of God, while His *blood* is the principle of confession. The blood cleanses us of our sins. The thing is, you can't just ask for forgiveness every now and then for "everything you have done." You must continually stay connected to Jesus and confess your sins on a daily basis. If you don't stay tuned in to Him daily – and confess your sins – you don't share in His salvation.

Let's stick to the basics. Spiritual exercise keeps us connected to God. Spiritual exercise, prayer, reading the Bible, attending church, fasting, you name it, this is what keeps us tuned in to Him. In other words, it opens our ears. It keeps us aware of God. Let me ask you: Are you aware of God's presence throughout your day? At work, at home, in traffic, how aware are you of God? Are you aware of His daily grace in your life?

FEBRUARY

Peace in God's Presence

The peace of God, which transcends all understanding, will guard your hearts and your minds in Christ Jesus. Philippians 4:7

Have you experienced true peace in your life, whether for ten seconds or half an hour? Have you reached some or other destination and thought, "This is where I want to stay forever"? There is such a place, and that is God. It is a place where peace surpasses all understanding and where you love all people, and forgive everyone, and can face anything. This is the most wonderful place to be.

That's where I want to be. I want to live in His presence. I want to work in His presence. I want to play with my children in His presence. And I want to handle stress and hold meetings in His presence. Morning, noon and night, I want to live in His presence. But for that to happen we need spiritual endurance. Matthew 24:13 says that the one who stands firm to the end will be saved.

To experience peace in God's presence we must daily humble ourselves before Him and ask for His guidance.

Strength from God

Being strengthened with all power according to His glorious might so that you may have great endurance and patience. Colossians 1:11

Why do we need strength from God? So that we can heal the sick? Make the dead come alive again? Or so that we can prophesy and it becomes true? Listen to what Paul says: so that we may have great endurance. Many times we are tempted to use this strength for our own honor and glory. But that's not what the Lord tells us – the more we persevere in faith, the closer we move towards Him.

Isn't that the most important reason? If we endure and get spiritually fit, we can do so much more for the Lord. We must be plugged in and stay plugged in to the Power Source. That's why God gave us His Holy Spirit. That's why He gave us spiritual disciplines, and that's basically why He gave us everything. He gives us everything we need to stay connected to Him, because our lives depend on it. This is where our successes lie. The closer we move towards God and grow in faith, the more we can mean something to this world.

Remain in the Vine

"Remain in Me, as I also remain in you.
No branch can bear fruit by itself; it must remain
in the vine. Neither can you bear
fruit unless you remain in Me." John 15:4

There is something important to keep in mind when you read this Scripture verse. Except for the strength that flows from us to the light, something else also happens to us. The cable that keeps us connected to God is burdened by the sin of this world, and tries to unplug us from God.

We've all experienced this, haven't we? The light needs power in order to shine, but sins try to separate us from the Power Source. It happens that power and strength flow from us, but we are still connected to the Source of the power. We must guard against letting the world separate us from our Power Source, because that can so easily happen. We read bad news, we watch the last ten minutes of a rugby match and we get upset, the guy in front of you in traffic annoys you … We must always stay connected, and be willing to let the Power flow through us to the world.

Our Loving God

"How can I give you up, Ephraim?
How can I hand you over, Israel?
My heart is changed within Me; all My compassion is aroused." Hosea 11:8

One of the first things that is very clear in the Bible is God's great love for people. God loved Adam and Eve so much that He met them right at the place where they were at. He walked with them in the Garden. God, the Almighty Creator of the universe, wants to have a relationship with us. Sometimes this is a bit much for us to process, and we shy away, much to our disadvantage, from a close and intimate relationship with the Lord.

God loves us too much to leave us where we are. We read about this love that He has for us in Genesis, Exodus, Leviticus, Numbers and Deuteronomy, and even in all the laws. Like God says here in Hosea, His compassion is aroused, and He will never leave us. We can doubt what people tell us, but God tells us how much He loves us. And not just love, but strong compassion not to be separated from us. What a wonderful thought!

Fear of the Lord

They said to Moses, "Speak to us yourself and we will listen. But do not have God speak to us or we will die." Exodus 20:19

Moses tells the people that God wants to have a relationship with them. Their reactions are astounding. They send Moses to go and talk to God alone. They don't want to go to the mountain. They don't want to meet with God. What would we have done in the same situation?

Say for instance we receive a message telling us that the Lord is going to be at a certain place and time this Wednesday to bring us a message. How many of us would make a great effort, in fact move mountains, to be there and hear what the Lord wants to tell us? How many people would send a messenger to report back on what He said?

Aren't we also a bit scared to meet Him face to face? Maybe we are scared because God knows everything about us. Isn't it time then to examine your life and remove all the things that make you feel ashamed in front of God?

To Reject God

The LORD told him: "Listen to all that the people are saying to you; it is not you they have rejected, but they have rejected Me as their king." 1 Samuel 8:7

God is our King and He asks us to serve Him. And like His people rejected Him in ancient times, we are also rejecting Him. We also rather want an earthly king. Someone we can see, because it's easier to negotiate with someone we can actually see.

Like God's people, we often also reject Him and serve other gods. Earthly gods are easier to serve; earthly gods are without rules and laws; earthly gods make us feel better about ourselves.

But earthly things divert us from the narrow path, steal eternal life from us and keep us imprisoned. Has the time not come to turn back to God? To turn back to the One who loves us with an everlasting love? To turn back to the One who gives us rest for our souls and where we can find abundant life? Today, say no to earthly gods that steal your everlasting peace.

Brotherly Love

Dear children, let us not love with words
or speech but with actions and in truth.
This is how we know that we belong
to the truth and how we set our hearts
at rest in His presence. 1 John 3:18-19

God loves the whole world and He sends you and me to also love others. This can sometimes be challenging because it occasionally happens that He sends you to love people who are different from you. Sometimes these people are so different to what you know that the command to love them is really difficult. But you've received so much, and God sends you to share this abundance.

Sometimes God sends you to people of another race or culture. God sends you to love people who are "different" from you, and that love starts by being friendly and polite. Get to know people's names, greet them by their names, and treat them with humanity. This might well be your first step towards a wonderful journey of brotherly love.

Get Involved

This is my prayer: that your love may abound more and more in knowledge and depth of insight. Philippians 1:9

The Lord often expects from us to get involved with others: involved in their heartache, in their crises, in their misery and poverty, and in their situation.

To love someone isn't just feeling something for them. Loving others means to help where you can, to support where you can. The greatest kind of love is to share the gospel with someone, to walk with them in order for them to receive the gospel of Christ.

God loves the whole world, and He sends us to love others; all people. John 3:16 is of course the most popular Scripture verse indicating God's love for the entire world, because "God so loved the world that He gave His one and only Son, that whoever believes in Him shall not perish but have eternal life." Do you know of someone with whom you could walk this road?

Our Salvation

"God so loved the world that He gave His one and only Son, that whoever believes in Him shall not perish but have eternal life." John 3:16

We briefly touched on this Scripture verse in yesterday's reading. Today we discuss it further. God's salvation of the world isn't just a quick and easy task to complete in one afternoon; it has come as far as 2,000 years. It started as early as when Israel was chosen as God's people. And what a difficult road this has been for them and the Savior who was born among them.

Jesus paid the ultimate price and died on a cross so that we could be saved from our sins. Can you see what a big deal our salvation is to God? God loved the world so much that from the beginning – from Genesis – He pointed Creation towards this moment. He sent His Son so that everybody on earth would not be condemned, but saved. If you don't feel like getting involved in someone else's salvation, think about this fact. Then it almost becomes impossible not to get involved.

Who Is God to You?

In the beginning God created the heavens and the earth. Genesis 1:1

What would your answer be if someone who knows nothing of God or Christianity asks you who this God of yours is? Many of us would perhaps think of these two things: God is the Creator of the universe and everything you see was made by Him. Or you might say that God is love.

God's story starts at creation. God created everything, above and beyond. What can we say about creation? God said that it was good. The only thing that wasn't good was that the man was alone; therefore God created a partner for Adam.

Creation was good, everything in nature worked well, the sun rose, the plants were watered and bore fruit, animals were born and things in creation ran smoothly.

God created something beautiful, and we are part of the greatness of creation.

What Does God Mean to You?

When the woman saw that the fruit of the tree was good for food and pleasing to the eye, and also desirable for gaining wisdom, she took some and ate it. She also gave some to her husband, who was with her, and he ate it. Genesis 3:6

Man destroyed God's once-perfect creation through sin and disobedience. Man chose to listen to the voice of the enemy, and through this gave in to sin, forfeiting his place in creation. Adam and Eve ate of the forbidden fruit and their eyes were opened. They realized that they were naked. They used fig leaves in an attempt to cover themselves. This is how the Fall came about, how their eyes were opened and how separation between God and people took place. There were consequences to their disobedience.

Man, who had everything in Paradise, lost everything because of his disobedience. The evil one got a foothold in creation and things started going wrong for man. This is an important point to remember, because this is the origin of God's plan of salvation for His people.

The Consequences of Sin

> To Adam He said, "Because you listened to your wife and ate fruit from the tree about which I commanded you, cursed is the ground because of you; through painful toil you will eat food from it all the days of your life. Genesis 3:17

The moment the Fall occurred, death came into the world. Everything was good, but at that moment when the enemy entered and polluted man, everything became an effort.

God told Adam in Genesis that the ground would now be cursed because the man allowed the woman to persuade him to eat of the fruit. From then on people would struggle to make a living. And at the end, people would return to the ground from which they were taken, becoming dust again. Life would be difficult. Few things would come easy.

The important thing to remember here is that it's not creation that's defective. It is people's sin that allowed suffering and heartache into the world. The good news is that it was from this point that God started His plan of salvation for us.

Full Assurance

In the beginning was the Word, and the Word was with God, and the Word was God. John 1:1

The Light that existed from the beginning couldn't be extinguished by the darkness.

God orchestrated our salvation by sending His Son, Jesus Christ. Jesus paid the price for you and me. He became flesh, He carried our sins and He died for us.

Now we have free access to God, we can all come to Him. We can say "Abba Father" and pray in the name of Jesus Christ. We can now know how it feels to receive forgiveness for our sins.

We have the full assurance that Christ took all the sins we've ever committed on Himself and paid the price in full. We can know for certain that we'll be with Him in heaven one day.

God's Plan of Restoration

"Go and make disciples of all nations, baptizing them in the name of the Father and of the Son and of the Holy Spirit, and teaching them to obey everything I have commanded you. And surely I am with you always, to the very end of the age." Matthew 28:19-20

God has a plan to restore things. Here God says to the people, "Become part of My plan of restoration. I'm not leaving things as they are now, all broken. You're going to become part of My triumphant procession."

This is what stands out about the Christian faith – God invites His people to become part of His plan of restoration. In Matthew 28:19 Jesus tells His disciples to go to all the nations and baptize them. He also says that they must always remember that He is with them, until the end of the age.

Our story also doesn't end after our salvation. Our story ends when we get to spend eternity in the presence of the Lord.

Our Conflicting Nature

Then God said, "Let us make mankind in Our image, in Our likeness, so that they may rule over the fish in the sea and the birds in the sky, over the livestock and all the wild animals, and over all the creatures that move along the ground." Genesis 1:26

This is probably one of the most conflicting things in a person's life. We are created in God's image, but we are so inclined to sin. Our sinful nature is a result of the Fall.

Parents sometimes don't want to believe that their precious babies are born in sin. They are so innocent! But let me tell you, I also experience this with my own children. I watch them fall. They are strong-willed, arrogant, disobedient, stubborn.

It is so important to bring up your children in the ways of the Lord. It sounds terrible, but we're all doomed to sin. For this reason you must guide your children and teach them to make the right decisions. Pray that godly knowledge will dictate their lives, not their sinful nature. They must know that only the Lord can save them. They must daily go to Him and ask Him to save and forgive them.

Persevere in Faith

"The one who stands firm to the end will be saved." Matthew 24:13

I often see how people are born again and then stop growing in their faith. Do you know how many people battle with their faith? Let me tell you, there are many churchgoers who are only one step away of falling back into sin. When you don't grow in your faith it becomes more and more difficult to persevere, especially when the demands of life get you down.

Faith is not sitting in church Sunday after Sunday. That's the easy part. Perseverance is being honest when it is easy to be dishonest, when you silently want to curse the motorist in front of you in traffic but don't, or proclaiming your faith when you would rather keep quiet. Every time you choose the easy way out it becomes all the more difficult to persevere the next time. Nobody said it would be easy, but the reward for perseverance is going to be out of this world. So next time you feel overcome by temptation, hang in there and ask the Lord to strengthen you.

Give Me Strength

We have this treasure in jars of clay to show that this all-surpassing power is from God and not from us. 2 Corinthians 4:7

Have you ever experienced the joy when God's power comes over you? You lie in bed at night and wonder, *Where did those words come from? It was amazing. How did I know I needed to phone that specific person? How did I know to send that message? How?*

The answer to all these questions is of course that it was God's power and strength at work in you.

God's power works in various ways in our lives. It gives us strength to help others on their faith journey. We also receive strength to endure on our own journey.

We as humans are sinful and weak in nature, and can't do much without His power and strength in our lives. The good news is that His power and strength are available to us every second of every day. Think about it – the power of the God who created the universe is available to you. That's amazing.

Love Each Other

This is my prayer: that your love may abound more and more in knowledge and depth of insight. Philippians 1:9

God invites us to live in love with others and with Him. God gave us the command to love others as we love ourselves. Others include our close family, our loved ones, our spouse, children, brothers and sisters and church family. But it doesn't stop here. Loving others also includes those people we don't know, people who are often a burden to us. We must also love them with the love of God.

If the Trinity is present in your life, fellowship and love will automatically also be present. We must love each other unconditionally. It is not always guaranteed, but mostly when we love others we also experience their love toward us.

The Bible says we must bear with each other, forgive each other, support each other, and pay attention to each other. We must treat each other in such a way that God's love truly shines through us.

Communicate Love

Has not the one God made you? You belong to Him in body and spirit. And what does the one God seek? Godly offspring. So be on your guard, and do not be unfaithful to the wife of your youth. Malachi 2:15

God takes the marriage vow very seriously. And therefore we must also view it with the necessary importance. Happy marriages are a blessing to all involved. Not only to the spouses, but also to the children, parents, even to friends and family.

One of the keys to a happy marriage is communication. If you communicate correctly with your spouse, he or she will be able to hear and feel that you love them, and then the marriage will flourish.

In unhappy marriages, spouses often don't feel loved. This can be because of several reasons and then it is time to find out how to speak your spouse's love language. And if your spouse is not speaking your love language, tell them what it is. Try it – you might just be surprised at the change in your marriage.

Say What You Mean

Do not lie to each other, since you have taken off your old self with its practices. Colossians 3:9

Good communication is so vital to any relationship. If we do not say what we mean clearly we have a break in communication. Often, in marriages it is easy for men and women to misunderstand each other. This is often the problem when emotions are involved. When you see your wife is clearly upset and you ask her what's wrong and she says, "Nothing" you know that you're in the dog box but you don't know why.

Men also communicate emotionally. When a man asks you, "Where are you going?" he's asking if you are going to bring him something to eat. When he says, "I missed you" he means there was nothing for him to eat. When he says, "I'm hungry" it means he's starving and when he doesn't say anything, he's probably died of hunger.

This is tongue-in-cheek, but it emphasizes the role emotions play in communication. Be sure to discuss this with your spouse so that you can work towards communicating more clearly.

Show Your Love

Let love and faithfulness never leave you;
bind them around your neck, write them on
the tablet of your heart. Proverbs 3:3

Communication not only involves what we say, but what we do. This physical side of communication involves deeds like when you take your wife's car in for a service, or when you cook dinner. It could be mowing the lawn, or when she brings you something to drink when you're working in the garden.

In other words, it can be anything you do for each other to show your love. And yes, of course it includes sex. But that's not the only thing.

When my spouse feels loved, I've succeeded in this type of communication. You and your spouse might spend ten hours a week talking, but still feel unloved.

The key to a successful marriage is to communicate your love successfully. It requires lots of practice, but it's worth it over and over again.

Make Time to Talk

Let your conversation be always full of grace, seasoned with salt, so that you may know how to answer everyone. Colossians 4:6

When you first meet your spouse and get married, to hear their voice is the highlight of your day. You share about your day and chat about the little things that happen. You laugh at the anecdotes you tell each other and you draw closer through the time you spend just talking.

After a while children arrive and work is stressful and sometimes everything becomes one big struggle for survival.

It is then that this type of communication becomes so important. It is vital to stay in touch with each other's lives. Make time to talk, and really listen to what the other person is saying. If you find that you can't talk to each other anymore without fighting, it's time to seek help. Don't lose each other in the chaos of life.

The Fruit of the Spirit

But the fruit of the Spirit is love,
joy, peace, forbearance, kindness,
goodness, faithfulness, gentleness
and self-control. Against such things
there is no law. Galatians 5:22-23

We all know this Scripture passage, but how many of us apply this to our lives? We don't need to be super-believers before we start living and acting in a way for others to see the fruit of the Spirit in our lives. It's a choice we make, and then we ask the strength of God to act in this way.

How many times do we just feel irritated with each other or just irritated in general and take it out on others? Does it really take that much effort to be decent and respectable towards others? Everybody experiences stress. If you feel that you really can't be decent to others at a specific point, go some place by yourself and ask God to give you inner peace.

Ask God every day for the strength to act and live as a child of His kingdom.

Tell the Truth

Each of you must put off falsehood and speak truthfully to your neighbor, for we are all members of one body. Ephesians 4:25

Sometimes we only stand up for the truth when it suits us. It mustn't be like this. The truth is always precious, beautiful and necessary. Truth is from God and shouldn't have any boundaries. But – and this is very important – truth must always go hand in hand with love.

It often happens that we hurt others with our words under the banner of "but it's the truth."

We must carefully distinguish between speaking the truth because it's the right thing to do and speaking the truth to hurt someone intentionally.

I'm not suggesting that you turn a blind eye to the wrongdoings of others, but examine your motives carefully before confronting them with the truth.

A lie can hurt, but truths told from a heart without love can hurt even more.

Serve the Lord

As a prisoner for the Lord, then, I urge you to live a life worthy of the calling you have received. Ephesians 4:1

Paul urges us to live a life worthy of our calling. We are made in God's image and therefore it's a given that we should feel motivated to proclaim His love.

Before you jump up, I'm not saying that we must all become missionaries in the field. That's certainly not intended for everyone. But you can for example show your love for God and others through your actions. We all know the saying that actions speak louder than words. And this is so true. You can demonstrate your love towards God through the way you treat others. Who knows, maybe that small act of kindness is the motivation someone needs to invite God into his or her life.

Don't ever think that your life doesn't matter. People see what you do – and God does too. Decide for yourself if this makes you glad or uneasy.

Pray for Wisdom

If any of you lacks wisdom, you should ask God, who gives generously to all without finding fault, and it will be given to you. James 1:5

Where does one find wisdom? You pray for it. You ask the Lord to guard your mouth and your emotions, and to teach you to act and communicate with wisdom towards everyone you meet. You ask the Lord to help you not to be overemotional or reckless with the truth. You can't just blindly make decisions and rush into situations. Even if it takes months or years in prayer before you act, wait for an answer from God.

Try this: Pray for one week for wise words and actively guard your mouth and the words you speak. I can assure you that your vocabulary will change within a week.

Pray for patience and ask God to help you to really listen to what others are saying. Allow God to help and guide you in every situation.

Don't Seek Revenge

Do not repay evil with evil or insult with insult. On the contrary, repay evil with blessing, because to this you were called so that you may inherit a blessing.

1 Peter 3:9

What is Paul actually saying here? If someone hurts you, don't hurt them in return. If someone insults you, don't also insult them. It seems like an easy enough task, but it is not always that simple.

It is only human to want to call for revenge. When we feel offended, we want justice to prevail. We don't want to leave judgment to God. And let's be honest, sometimes He just takes His time. We want to see results *now*.

What we forget is that God sees the entire picture – He knows exactly how everything fits together. He knows when the time is right, and He also knows the blessings that lie in forgiveness rather than in condemnation.

Payback often causes a lot of pain. So no matter how difficult it is not to judge, leave it to God. You must forgive and bless others through God's love.

Forgive like Jesus

Jesus said, "Father, forgive them, for they do not know what they are doing." Luke 23:34

To add to yesterday's devotion, I want to say something more about forgiveness. Can you imagine what went through Jesus' mind while He was hanging on the cross: anger, pain, heartache, forsaken by God? And what does He say? Forgive these people because they do not know what they're doing.

I want to focus on the part "they do not know what they are doing." It is sometimes genuinely the case. I don't want to talk about people who intentionally hurt, betray or offend you. But sometimes people just don't realize how hurtful their words and actions can be. And sometimes they're so involved in their own business that your hurt just passes them by. Their "jokes" are like daggers in your heart, but you laugh and hide your pain. And what does the Lord say? Forgive them, free yourself from the pain. Give everything over to Him, and forgive them. It will be to your own benefit.

Live in Love

I ask that we love one another.
And this is love: that we walk in obedience
to His commands. As you have heard
from the beginning, His command is
that you walk in love. 2 John 1:5-6

It's not hard to open the Bible anywhere and read about God's love for us. It's easy to tell our loved ones that we love them, or at least the people we like. But God says that we must walk in love. And to love one another. Everyone. Now it becomes a bit more difficult, right? There are many people we don't like or who don't like us. How on earth are we supposed to love everyone!

It requires a lot of perseverance to keep on loving other people. But if you get it right, you'll find that it becomes easier. Are you an example of loving others? Do you try to live in love with others? It is worth it, because the more you live in love, the more love you will receive.

MARCH

Be There for One Another

Help each other and say to their companions, "Be strong!" Isaiah 41:6

We know that God loves us, and that He only wants what is best for us. He wants us to have the same relationship with other people. We must love, support and encourage one another.

When we support each other, life is so much easier. It's good to know that someone is looking out for you, that someone will help you up when you stumble or reprimand you when you stray from the narrow path.

It is often easy to come to church on a Sunday and be friendly and supportive towards others. But it is a whole different story when we're at home, when we're tired and don't feel like putting our best foot forward. Now put yourself in someone else's shoes – wouldn't you appreciate a bit of encouragement in such times? Wouldn't someone else's shoulder give you the strength to face tomorrow? Love others and be a helper to your neighbor every day.

A Family Loves One Another

You are also members of His household. Ephesians 2:19

A home is supposed to be a loving place. And in most cases this is true. You feel safe when you're with your family. After all, these are the people who not only know your good side, but have also seen your worst side. It is among your own people and family where you experience unconditional love for the first time.

We are also part of a bigger family, the household of God. We are all brothers and sisters in God's love. Like an earthly family protects one another against the world, likewise our spiritual brothers and sisters should protect each other against the attacks of the evil one.

We must intercede for each other, support each other and love each other unconditionally. And when someone strays, we must lovingly guide them back to the safety of our godly family.

Serve Each Other in Love

Let us not love with words or speech but with actions and in truth. This is how we know that we belong to the truth and how we set our hearts at rest in His presence. 1 John 3:18-19

The Bible often reminds us to carry each other's burdens, to forgive each other, to bear with each other, and to laugh and cry together.

Even more important than all these "each other" commands is that we do everything in love. Often it is not what we do for others that count, but with how much love we do it. One soon realizes when someone seemingly supports you, but doesn't do it out of love. They just do it to say that they've done something.

When God's love lives in us it isn't an effort to really be there for others. In fact, it is pleasant to support and lovingly encourage others.

Be someone who shows your love for others in practical ways. Don't help and support just to get it over with. Love others sincerely.

Love One Another

"A new command I give you: Love one another. As I have loved you, so you must love one another." John 13:34

When I read this Scripture verse I immediately think of marriage. Why do we get married? It is not something we have to think about. We get married because we love each other.

Give this Scripture verse ten or twenty years down the line to a husband and wife when things have changed; when your husband or wife is not "the same" as when you got married. You can't say that you were madly in love with someone, but that everything changed the moment you got married. Perhaps it's not your husband or wife who has changed, but rather yourself.

This Scripture verse doesn't have to be so challenging. Men, love your wives. Wives, love your husbands like Jesus loves us. This is the bottom line: Jesus says we must love one another, and it's a command. Jesus loves us, and we must love one another, as easy as that.

Be a Disciple

"Follow Me." Mark 2:14

Jesus wasn't concerned about what people would think of the disciples He chose. The disciples who were called by Jesus immediately followed Him. Think of Matthew. When Jesus said, "Follow Me," he followed without hesitation.

Too often we are concerned about our reputation and what people are going to say or think.

We can't see other people's hearts like Jesus sees them; we can just try to make an assumption based on how they act and what they say. We must do our best to surround ourselves with people who say "Yes" to Jesus without wavering.

Even when we think they aren't high in stature in society, we must try to choose like Jesus chose. Besides, there is nothing more important than the approval of our heavenly Father.

Where Do You Come From?

"Nazareth! Can anything good come from there?" Nathanael asked. John 1:46

Nathanael wondered if it was worth it to follow Jesus because He came from Nazareth, and according to him nothing good came from there.

Aren't we also like that sometimes? Oh no, not *that* place. Nothing good comes from there. Or what about the in-laws: "Where does he come from? What does he do? … A what? … A pastor? Shame, my girl, I'll have to care for you for the rest of my life ..."

Have you ever felt insulted by someone? Your family? Your background? That's exactly what Nathanael did, because he questioned how anything good could come from Nazareth. In other words: Joseph, Mary, Jesus? How can anyone love someone from Nazareth?

Don't be like Nathanael and be blinded by face value. We must love one another the way we are, not because of where we come from.

Live Life to the Full

If we love one another, God lives in us and His love is made complete in us. This is how we know that we live in Him and He in us. 1 John 4:12-13

These Scripture verses stretch one to love others like Jesus loves us. The verses have something beautiful about them, because Jesus said that if we love one another, people will see that we are His children.

Who do you think are the most important people in my life who should know this truth? My children. They don't see Jesus' love when I preach, they see Jesus' love in the way I treat them and their mother.

Many pastors' children don't want anything to do with the church. Maybe it's because Dad preaches one kind of love from the pulpit and shows another kind at home. Many parents are in church every Sunday, but their children don't want anything to do with the gospel. Perhaps they show love on a Sunday, but are different from Monday to Saturday. We must live in such a way that others can see Jesus' love in our lives every day.

Dealing with Conflict

"If your brother or sister sins, go and point out their fault, just between the two of you." Matthew 18:15

There are two ways of handling conflict. You can deal with it by becoming bitter, mad, vengeful and by screaming and shouting, or by staying calm. I've seen what bitterness can do to a marriage; it causes deep pain. Some people are like this. They only remember the hurt; they make their jibes and they want to break down, because that's what the other person did. But I've also seen marriages where love triumphed, and where conflict was resolved in a loving way, and that's a wonderful experience.

Jesus didn't say that we will never experience conflict. But He did say we must treat each other with love.

Jesus chooses to be friendly and to care for others, to forgive and live from the basis of that forgiveness. It's a choice. You must choose how you want to live, how you're going to love like Jesus. It's your choice – how will you live?

Loving Others as Yourself

You, my brothers and sisters, were called to be free. Serve one another humbly in love. For the entire law is fulfilled in keeping this one command: "Love your neighbor as yourself." Galatians 5:13-14

People can sometimes rip one another apart over the most trivial things. I've seen how church members attack one another over church politics and dogmatism; how men and women destroy each other over something insignificant.

The freedom that we read about in today's Scripture is not the freedom to attack others and say and do what we like. It must rather be the freedom to deal with your emotions first before you hurt or attack someone. It's the freedom to create a platform of unconditional love and acceptance. You mustn't use your freedom as an excuse to sin.

People won't always agree with you on everything, but Jesus' love calls us to always treat each other with love and respect, no matter what. Ask God to help you to treat others in such a way that they can see Jesus in you.

Encourage Each Other

Therefore encourage one another and build each other up, just as in fact you are doing. 1 Thessalonians 5:11

We all want to be in relationships where we get support and hear that we are doing well. It could be in your marriage or in any other relationship.

Life passes by so quickly. Perhaps you still wanted to tell your wife that she's a good mother, say to your friend what her love and care mean to you, or thank a colleague for their support. For some or other reason you didn't tell them, and then found it was too late. Maybe you wanted to apologize to someone for something you did, or confess your sins and shortcomings, but kept quiet for too long.

Don't find yourself in a place of regret. Say what you want to say, but ask God's guidance at all times so that you don't say things that hurt, but rather things that encourage and build up.

Our Desires

Enjoy what you have rather than desiring what you don't have. Ecclesiastes 6:9 NLT

Often when we hear the word *desire* we link it to something negative, to something that we want but can't have. And it's often also true that we desire things like more money, a bigger house, a new job, well-behaved children, and nicer holidays.

We as Christians must be wary of desiring things because it often blinds us to what we already have. It makes us forget about the abundant blessings we have received. We have money to provide for our basic needs, we have a roof over our heads, we have a job, our children aren't sick, and at least we can afford a holiday.

If you really want to desire something, why not desire a deeper relationship with God? A loving relationship with your fellow men? Desire to be the best parent you can possibly be. To desire is not always bad, it just depends on what you desire. Are your desires in line with God's will for your life?

Delight Yourself in the Lord

Trust in the LORD and do good; dwell
in the land and enjoy safe pasture.
Take delight in the LORD, and He will give
you the desires of your heart. Psalm 37:3-4

The Bible clearly tells us that the Lord will give us the desires of our hearts. Yes, but there's a catch: If we delight ourselves in Him, He will grant our desires.

The thing is that if we delight ourselves in Him and trust Him, our hearts will be changed as well as the things that we desire. We will desire a deeper relationship with the Lord, or to be a better person; in other words, our desires will be pleasing to the Lord.

If we strongly desire to be closer to God, the things of the world won't tempt us anymore. We'll know the joy of a deep relationship with God, because that will be our biggest desire.

Know What You're Asking

James and John, the sons of Zebedee, came to Jesus. "Teacher," they said, "we want You to do for us whatever we ask … Let one of us sit at Your right and the other at Your left in Your glory." Mark 10:35, 37

James and John thought they were just asking a simple question. They thought they were asking something that Jesus would easily give them. One day in His glory, the one wanted to sit at His right and the other at His left. According to them, there was nothing wrong with their request.

However, their request was very superficial. They wanted to be in control of the kingdom – at that stage they had no idea that His kingdom is not an earthly kingdom. They still wanted to fight with swords and shields and be the heroes on earth.

What would you ask Jesus if He stood right in front of you? Would you also choose earthly fame and glory like James and John? Or would you ask for what will matter in His kingdom? Our only desire must be a life in service to the Lord. Then He will give us whatever we ask for.

Earthly Needs

Jesus was in the stern, sleeping on a cushion.
The disciples woke Him and said to Him,
"Teacher, don't You care if we drown?" Mark 4:38

We seem to be drowning: the economy, gas prices, interest rates, loans, the house, children, exams, this and that – around us a storm is raging. In the midst of it Jesus says, "Relax, it's all earthly desires."

The disciples jumped up at the first sign of the boat seemingly going down. And what does Jesus do? He simply stands up, speaks, and the storm passes. He says, "Do you still not trust Me?" It is almost as if He wants to say that these superficial things are not a challenge for Him. "I rather want to address your deepest being." Jesus is always more concerned about our spiritual blindness and inability to trust Him.

What is your deepest longing? Is it a happy marriage, to grow closer to Jesus, to know Him better? Whatever it is, take it to Him.

A Meaningful Life

"Not everyone who calls out to Me,
'Lord! Lord!' will enter the Kingdom of Heaven.
Only those who actually do the will of My
Father in heaven will enter." Matthew 7:21 NLT

We all want to accomplish something in life. We want to be "discovered," and we want someone to value our potential. We mistakenly think that someone else must discover it. Actually nobody needs to discover this potential, because it's already in us. We must just use it.

We mustn't be blinded by earthly fame and glory. We know that we've succeeded in life when we follow the will of our Father in heaven. We know that we're successful when we build His kingdom on earth and win souls for His glory.

On which roll of honor will your name appear? On the earthly one where nothing has eternal value, or will your name be written in the Book of Life because you gave everything for His kingdom?

What Is in the Heart

The heart is deceitful above all things and beyond cure. Who can understand it? Jeremiah 17:9

Nobody else knows what's going on inside you, and nobody can change a person's heart, besides God of course. The Lord looks at a person's heart and thoughts. The Lord knows what our motives are. The human heart is generally deceitful.

Ask yourself, "What are the longings of my heart today before the Lord?" You're going to hear *There's a storm raging, it's chaos here.* You're only going to hear negative things. The Lord says you must come to Him to delve deeper into your own thoughts, motives and heart's desires.

Be still and reveal your heart before God – not because of Him, but because of yourself. Don't let your heart deceive you. Be honest with yourself and with God. Then you'll grow in the life He intended for you.

God Knows You

You know when I sit and when I rise; You perceive my thoughts from afar. Psalm 139:2

The Lord knows you, and He sees you right where you are. He wants to have a relationship with you. He can heal our innermost being. His kingdom can give meaning to our lives and He can help us not to pursue the meaningless things in life. He meets us right where we are.

When I did the exercise one day of just being quiet and waiting in stillness before God, I discovered it is right there that the story of life is written – all the psalms from David, all the books of the Bible.

It is *there* where you become still and meet with your soul, and find that only God can satisfy you. You will see that you can't live from bread alone, but from every word that comes from Him.

Open up your heart and allow God to touch your life and make it His.

The Jesus Prayer

"When you pray, do not keep on babbling like pagans." Matthew 6:7

There are many Christians who pray the Jesus Prayer. It goes as follows: "O Lord Jesus Christ, Son of God, have mercy on me, a sinner."

It's not a difficult prayer, but a very powerful one. It is a combination of three prayers in the Bible where someone prayed for his sins, someone else called out to Jesus and a blind man asked Jesus to have mercy on him. It is therefore not a prayer that you will find word for word in the Bible.

This prayer can reach down deep into your soul. When you pray, "O Lord Jesus Christ, Son of God, have mercy on me, a sinner," you begin to realize that you only need an encounter with Christ to receive His mercy and grace. You start to see that you don't need all these worldly and superficial things to experience fulfillment, because you have the living Lord Jesus in your life and that's all that matters.

Love for Self

"'Love your neighbor as yourself.' There is no commandment greater than these." "Well said, Teacher," the man replied. "You are right in saying that God is one and there is no other but Him."

Mark 12:29-32

One of the things that make life worth living is loving others and being loved. If you love yourself you are saying that you love life: You love your body, you love your relationships, your finances, your emotions; you love everything. That's what it means to love yourself. If you love yourself, you can follow God with your whole being.

God calls you to follow Him with your whole life. This "whole life" of ours, the be all and end all, is the following: We want joy, happiness, fulfillment, and life. Each one of us has an instinctive urge for survival. We have this instinct that says *I will fight for life, I want life, I long for happiness, I want fulfillment on earth.* May our lives on this earth not be worthless, pointless, and just routine.

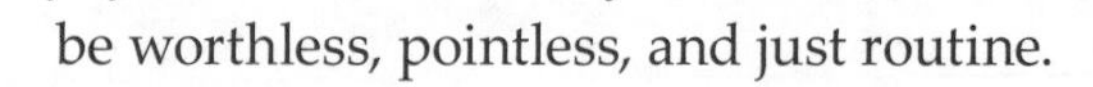

The Wisdom of Ecclesiastes

> I applied myself to the understanding of wisdom, and also of madness and folly, but I learned that this, too, is a chasing after the wind. Ecclesiastes 1:17

Everything is a chasing after the wind, but what is this chasing? I'm searching for life. This fulfillment differs from person to person. Something that I find fulfilling might mean nothing to you, or something that you dislike might make me happy.

It can also happen that the things that are important to you change from time to time. Suppose you were always a big football supporter over weekends, but nowadays you would rather mow the lawn on a Saturday. What does it mean? What are you going to do to get your *joie de vivre* back?

It's not the end of the world if you don't support football anymore, but what happens when you lose your fervor for the church and spiritual matters? What must you do to get your spiritual life back on track? The only answer is to humble yourself in prayer before God. Only He can help you find your passion for life again so that everything doesn't feel like a chasing after the wind.

Recharge Your Batteries

If we hope for what we do not yet have,
we wait for it patiently. Romans 8:25

Not everyone finds it easy to persevere in faith. People lose their commitment for the things of the Word, for different reasons.

Often a lack of passion in your Christian life is a sign of physical exhaustion. If you neglect the one, it is only natural that the other one will also be neglected. What must you do to regain your fervor for the Word? There are those who bury themselves in sport, others go shopping and some people just need time to relax with a friend or go fishing.

It is good to recharge your batteries every now and then in our busy and hectic lives – especially when our physical tiredness prevents us from giving everything to the Lord. We must, however, remember that whatever we do, to do it in honor of God.

We must also not regard our physical pleasures too highly because they can eventually keep us away from God.

Your Daily Work

How joyful are those who fear the Lord – all who follow His ways! You will enjoy the fruit of your labor. How joyful and prosperous you will be!

Psalm 128:1-2 NLT

For many people their work is their life. They enjoy their work and feel that they make an important contribution in their profession. This satisfaction can later become completely distorted. Then they only work for the recognition of others. Some people even neglect their own families.

It is not wrong to work – God has ordained work and He says in the Bible that we will reap the fruit of our labor. We can work and enjoy it; we can work and glorify Him at the same time.

Review your work schedule. Do you have time to yourself, do you have time for your loved ones, and do you have time to wholeheartedly serve the Lord? If your answer is "no" to any one of these questions, it is time to ask the Lord to help you set your priorities straight.

The Love of Money

The love of money is a root of all kinds of evil. Some people, eager for money, have wandered from the faith and pierced themselves with many griefs. 1 Timothy 6:10

For many people this is a sensitive subject. But read carefully what the Scripture verse says: The love of money is the root of all kinds of evil. It is OK to have money, it is OK to save money, and it is even OK to be wealthy.

Unfortunately, money becomes a safety net for many people. They don't trust God for their provision, they only trust in money. And then everything starts revolving around making more and more money. People often want more money to be regarded as important in society.

Don't make money your idol. Work hard and live within your means. Always trust God to provide and care for you. You can have all the money in the world, but if you don't have God you have nothing. What does your relationship with God, and with money, look like? Discuss this with God in prayer.

The Promise of Life

"I am the gate; whoever enters through Me will be saved. They will come in and go out, and find pasture." John 10:9

Look carefully at this picture: Jesus' dream for you is to always find green pastures with Him. But it goes even further than our daily needs. This is our promise of eternal life. We hear something of peace and rest. Jesus is our only salvation. He is the only entrance we'll ever need.

Life is hectic; people are sly; cursing and swearing are the order of the day; affairs, dishonesty and lies are rampant. The world and the church clash.

It is here that Jesus tells you to come to Him to find green pastures. With Him we find eternal life and He will fulfill our needs. He allows you to enjoy life, sport, holidays, work and marriage. Surrender your heart to Him, then you will experience life in abundance.

Fountains of Joy

With You is the fountain of life;
in Your light we see light. Psalm 36:9

When God provides for us we can be sure that we will receive abundant joy from His hand.

God wants you to be happy; God is pleased when we laugh. He likes it when we feel truly alive. He says we must drink from the fountain of joy. With Him is the fountain of life – the beginning, the origin. In His light we see light; in other words, you only see darkness when you don't look at things through His light.

Don't be afraid to approach God with the darkness of your sin. His light and forgiveness will remove all sin and banish all darkness.

Choose today to say yes to His invitation and experience for yourself what it is to drink from the fountain of life.

Say No to the Enemy

"The thief comes only to steal and kill and destroy." John 10:10

What does the thief do? He spreads lies about your hobbies and leisure activities. Firstly, he's going to make you feel guilty, and then he'll convince you that you need more relaxation time. You can go fishing every weekend and miss a few church services, as long as you enjoy it.

The moment you get away from your guilt he'll whisper in your ear again: "You're a bad person. Why aren't you in church?" And then you feel guilty all over again.

If you don't allow Christ into your life, the indulgences become the sins. When you can't carry on and need some time out, you indulge yourself and then feel guilty again for the next six months. But if you know in Christ that it is OK and that He wants you to socialize, play sports and relax, then you realize He is part of that and you find life and rest.

Life in Abundance

"I have come that they may have life, and have it to the full." John 10:10

What is Jesus' plan? Life in abundance. What does abundance mean? In your twenties you are still exploring and discovering life; you do all kinds of exciting things and try out everything. You're also looking for "the one" with whom you want to spend the rest of your life. When you turn thirty you get a rude awakening because you realize that the things that were so important in your twenties are not so important anymore. When you reach forty you discover a lot of other priorities that you hadn't thought about before. And so it continues as you grow older.

You start to wonder about the meaning of it all, what and whom can you trust, because your priorities keep changing. Many people take religion extremely seriously and think that God now doesn't allow us any fun – everything is all of a sudden sinful. But God calls you to Himself. And even if your view on life and priorities change, God still wants to give you a life of abundance.

Come and Rest

"Come to Me, all you who are weary and burdened, and I will give you rest." Matthew 11:28

What a wonderful invitation from Jesus! For many people, their burdens feel overwhelming. They can't put one foot in front of the other anymore, because worldly things are suffocating them.

But Jesus tells us to give everything that overwhelms and bothers us to Him. He will carry it for us. He will carry it on His shoulders and free us from the burden. Don't let anything stand in your way of surrendering your burdens to Him.

Nowhere do we find a more wonderful invitation than this one. Jesus doesn't want us to go through life feeling burdened and exhausted; He invites us to bring our troubles to Him and leave them there.

Have you given your troubles over to Him and experienced the feeling of freedom? We truly serve a God who cares for us. Do you still battle to let go?

Fishers of Men

"Therefore go and make disciples of all nations, baptizing them in the name of the Father and of the Son and of the Holy Spirit." Matthew 28:19

God loves the whole world and He sends us to proclaim His message of love to the world. We also read in Acts 1:8, "You will receive power when the Holy Spirit comes on you; and you will be My witnesses in Jerusalem, and in all Judea and Samaria, and to the ends of the earth." With this, He tells us that He will give us the strength to proclaim the gospel.

It is a biblical command to go out and love others. We all know that, but the effort is the challenge, because it doesn't happen by itself. For many people it is difficult to talk about the Lord.

We battle to deal with the demands of life as it is; we don't have time to talk to strangers about the Lord. It is a deliberate decision to be available so God can use you to love the world.

Give Freely

"Freely you have received; freely give." Matthew 10:8

Jesus spoke these words to His disciples and they are so true for us today. He says we have freely received all these things – mercy, life – and we must now give them away for free to a lost world longing for His love. Few things in life are free. We must work for what we want and often make sacrifices to get it.

Even if it seems like we're going to get something for free, it's not the case – there are always hidden costs or a catch somewhere. But Jesus says that we've all received these things for free, and must also give them freely.

Isn't it wonderful that we've received the biggest gift in the world for free? Without any catches or hidden costs. So share this gift with the world today.

God Will Use You

There were four men with leprosy at the entrance of the city gate. They said to each other, "Why stay here until we die?" 2 Kings 7:3

In the Old Testament we read how the Arameans attacked Israel and besieged Samaria. The town residents were trapped without any food and water. Then four people with leprosy decided to go and ask for food from the Aramean army. They felt like they were starving to death in any case so they had nothing to lose.

The Lord, however, uses the efforts of these desperate men to save a whole city. The Lord caused the Arameans to hear the sounds of chariots and horses and a great army. It made them think that they were under attack and they fled. All the people of Samaria were saved.

Sometimes you think you do something just for yourself, or you don't really want to do it, but it could just be what the Lord uses to make big things happen. So go out today and do that thing that scares you. God might just do great and mighty things through you.

APRIL

Share Your Gifts and Talents

Share with the Lord's people
who are in need. Romans 12:13

We've read about how the four lepers decided to go to the Aramean camp to ask for food. At the camp they saw that all the Aramean soldiers had left everything and fled. They left behind food, silver, gold and clothes. The Arameans even left their horses and donkeys.

While the lepers were celebrating over what they'd found, they realized that the people in the town were probably also perishing from hunger and misery. They decided to go and tell the town's people the wonderful news.

Aren't we also sometimes tempted to keep our gifts and talents to ourselves? If something good happens to you today, share it with someone; it might mean a lot to him or her.

God has given you much and He expects you to share the good things you have with His children.

Accept the Good Gifts

In Him you have been enriched in every way – with all kinds of speech and with all knowledge. 1 Corinthians 1:5

There are many skeptical people in the world: people who believe that nothing good will ever happen to them, people who always expect the worst. It is often because of their pessimism that they are blind to the wonderful care and goodness of the Lord.

God blessed His people abundantly in biblical times, and He still blesses us today. Do you have food on the table, a roof over your head, clothes to wear? Can you live where you want, read what you want and worship where you want? Are you free to practice your Christianity with other believers? These are all blessings and privileges from God's hand. In many parts of the world people don't have these privileges.

Open your eyes today to the wonderful gifts that God gives us, and thank Him for the life that you have. You are truly blessed in abundance.

Be Obedient

We must obey God rather
than human beings! Acts 5:29

We've already seen that we are supposed to share God's love with the world, but we don't do it. Why do we obey so many commands, but are still disobedient when it comes to this one?

We are often scared that people will fight with us, or won't like what we have to say. We are scared of conflict and being cornered.

Still God expects us to be obedient. Even when we don't feel like it and have to be good to people who reject us, be obedient to God's command and share His good news with others. It is sometimes as simple as telling someone that the blessings you've received are gifts from the Father's hand.

Don't be so worried about what other people think. Their approval doesn't really matter. We must rather be concerned about what God thinks of us, and if we are honoring Him with our obedience.

Choose Life

In the way of righteousness there is life;
along that path is immortality. Proverbs 12:28

How easy is it to choose Jesus? For some people it's an easy decision, but for others it's a difficult one, with many earthly sacrifices.

People know that there will be certain consequences when they choose the Lord. They know they'll probably lose some of their friends. They may well change the way they talk and what they read. Many things will change for them.

Your conversion will cost you something, but the reward that awaits you is worth sacrificing all earthly things. When you obey the Lord, you receive something that no human relationship can give: eternal life.

In terms of earthly possessions it will feel like you're losing a lot, but when you look at the eternal reward you'll see that nothing compares to this decision.

Are you going to be obedient today and choose life?

The Price of Our Salvation

In Him we have redemption through His blood,
the forgiveness of sins, in accordance
with the riches of God's grace. Ephesians 1:7

God paid a big price for us. Jesus gave His life to save us and establish our salvation. He asks then that we share this wonderful news with the rest of the world.

For many of us it takes guts to go out and tell someone about Jesus. But have you thought about the courage it required of Jesus to give up His life? Yes, it takes effort to go and proclaim the gospel, but if we look at the big picture and Jesus' sacrifice, what we have to sacrifice looks insignificant.

Ask God's help next time your hands start sweating and your mouth dries up at the thought of telling someone about Him.

Ask God to take away your fear for people and to share His message of love and mercy courageously with the whole world.

Bought at a Price

You were bought at a price; do not become slaves of human beings. 1 Corinthians 7:23

To become "slaves of human beings" can mean various things, one of which is to be constantly concerned about what others might say and think of us. But God says we were bought at a price and we are free. Accordingly, we are free from what others think of us.

We must stop being afraid to live out our Christianity; we must stop being scared of doing the right thing in times where it is becoming more and more difficult to stand up for what's right. We must also not be afraid of loving others unconditionally with the love of Jesus – even though the world doesn't understand this love.

We must pray that the Lord will change our hearts and make us true instruments of His love for lost people. We aren't here just for our own survival. We are here to love people like Jesus loves them, and to bring them the message of God's salvation and love.

Who Is It About?

For what we preach is not ourselves, but Jesus Christ as Lord, and ourselves as your servants for Jesus' sake. 2 Corinthians 4:5

Will this coming week be just about you? It is a choice, not a question. It is a plan, a strategy that you plan and work out in your heart and say, "Lord, I want to live for You. You love the whole world and You send me to also love others. Where can I show Your love to lost people?"

The choice about how you're going to live is yours, but let me ask you one question: How would you feel when the year is coming to an end and you realize that you've done nothing or meant nothing to someone else? You may have excuses like you were too busy or didn't have time. But do you think the Lord will accept your excuses? Do you think He'll like it when you've put yourself first the entire year? Everything in life is about Him, about His glory and honor, and about carrying out His message of love. You are here to be obedient to Jesus. Don't look back at the end of the year and realize you've done nothing for others.

A Godly Fight

Though we live in the world, we do not wage war as the world does. 2 Corinthians 10:3

Paul says that although we dwell in earthly bodies, we don't wage war with human weapons. There are two types of weapons: human and spiritual. Examples of human weapons include knowledge, degrees, diplomas, money and an address book with all the right numbers in case of an emergency. With these human weapons you can only fight human fights.

What do spiritual weapons look like? These weapons change hearts and stop arguments. These weapons allow you access to the divine. These weapons are eternal; they are Spirit and they are godly. Which weapon do you take up when you leave your house every day? Let me tell you, most people pray for these weapons: "Oh, Lord, today's meeting, today's work, today's contract, today's sale, and today's employees."

Don't be blinded by today when you ask for help. Think about matters of eternal value and ask for the weapons of the Spirit.

Sent by God

Then I heard the voice of the Lord saying,
"Whom shall I send? And who will go for Us?"
And I said, "Here am I. Send me!" Isaiah 6:8

God loves the whole world and He wants to use His children to carry out His message of love. We must be like Isaiah, always ready and willing to be used by God. We must also say without hesitation, "Here am I. Send me!"

We are all called by God to be His messengers. When you meet someone in need, do you share God's message or do you flee? Allow God's Spirit to flow through you, and allow Him to guide you to be His messenger of love and mercy.

We mustn't be hesitant to be His messengers. Think about it – you might just be in the right place at the right time to lead someone into God's kingdom.

Don't let the chance pass you by because you pretended not to hear God's command. Say "Yes" immediately and listen to the Spirit's promptings in your soul.

God’s Love in You

“My command is this: Love each other as I have loved you.” John 15:12

God loves the whole world and He sends us to love the world, too. Part of that love is to tell others about God’s message of love and redemption. We can’t say we love our fellow men if we don’t tell them about the salvation found in the Lord.

Because God loves us, we’ve also received His grace. Therefore, we must also be merciful to the people we meet. We mustn’t judge them, but rather show them mercy when they sin against us, especially when they ask for mercy.

God’s love for us must be visible in our love for others. When we truly love Him, we’ll make disciples for Him without wavering.

Do you think your fellow human beings can see God’s love in you?

Be Baptized

Whoever believes and is
baptized will be saved. Mark 16:16

The context of this Scripture verse speaks about being sent to love others and the great commission. Unfortunately, this very Scripture verse creates a lot of discord, not just in the church, but also in families.

Instead of going out and making disciples and seeing people being saved, we would rather argue about whether we should be baptized as a baby, or as an adult, or more than once, or whatever. Therefore, this command isn't carried out, because we don't want to cause more division, we want to see the world being saved. We want to tell the world about Jesus, not cause an argument.

It's important that we do what God has called us to do by going out and telling others the good news of salvation and new life that are available through Christ. Don't let confusion about the issue of baptism stop you from doing this.

The Great Commission

"Therefore go and make disciples of all nations, baptizing them in the name of the Father and of the Son and of the Holy Spirit, and teaching them to obey everything I have commanded you." Matthew 28:19-20

Let's take a look at the second part of this verse "teaching them to obey everything I have commanded you."

If you were to summarize the greatest lesson of Jesus' life, what would it be? Love. We must love each other. Jesus' love doesn't throw stones; it is a forgiving love, a love that cares for others, a love that is not bound by tradition or culture.

The command to go out and teach other people is in fact a command to love others like God loves us.

Tell others about this boundless love, this love that doesn't condemn. A love that doesn't condemn is a love that accepts despite differences.

Baptism Is a Sign of Salvation

"Therefore go and make disciples of all nations, baptizing them in the name of the Father and of the Son and of the Holy Spirit." Matthew 28:19

Maybe we must look at what being baptized means to us. Being baptized is a sign that we accept God's love and salvation, and are allowed into Christ's church community. Baptism is a visible sign of a person's salvation through Christ.

People like to make all kinds of rules and regulations, and woe to the one who doesn't agree with them. In these rules the true meaning of baptism sometimes gets lost. We want to tie down a sacrament of God with rules in order to control it. But we can't control God.

Look past the issue of baptism – being baptized as an infant or an adult or more than once – and look at what God has taught us about baptism. Baptism is an outward display of the new life that we have because of Christ.

Invite the Outsiders

Then Jesus said, "When you give a luncheon or dinner, do not invite your friends, your brothers or sisters, your relatives, or your rich neighbors; if you do, they may invite you back and so you will be repaid. But when you give a banquet, invite the poor, the crippled, the lame, the blind." Luke 14:12-13

God will reward those people who invite the poor, who cannot repay them, to their banquets. In the Scripture passage Jesus reprimands the Pharisees of His time. They believed that those who were crippled or disabled were cursed by God. They only had one rule and that was to invite only good, righteous, wealthy, and holy people.

We must not be like the Pharisees. We must never disregard people because they can't do something for us. Or even worse, because we are afraid of what others might think if we help them.

God sees what we do. He will reward us if we have compassion on the outcasts in society. Make space today at your table for someone who can't invite you back.

Less Than Perfect

"Mephibosheth, grandson of your master, will always eat at my table." 2 Samuel 9:10

Mephibosheth was Jonathan's son. He fell when he was a baby and as a result was lame in both feet. David invited Mephibosheth to his table. He told him that there was a place for him at the table.

Mephibosheth answered, "What is your servant, that you should notice a dead dog like me?" Even in David's time one only invited a select few to one's table, but David didn't care about that. He invited Mephibosheth to eat with him – for the rest of his life.

That's exactly what Jesus tells us to do. He gives us a new set of table manners, together with a new heart. Jesus says that whoever we invite will say a lot about what is in our hearts. It will speak of our love for our neighbor. It will indicate whether we include or exclude.

What do the people around your table look like? Do you include or exclude?

The Prodigal Son

"'Your brother has come,' he replied, 'and your father has killed the fattened calf because he has him back safe and sound.'" Luke 15:27

We all know the parable of the Prodigal Son who wanted all of his inheritance from his father. He wastes everything and humbly returns to his father's house. The father is overjoyed at his son's return, but the older brother does not share his father's sentiment. He is mad and refuses to attend the feast.

Aren't we also like the older brother sometimes? We feel offended about things we think we deserve and don't get.

Jesus wants us to look past these grievances and celebrate the fact that the brother returned. Instead of being bitter about what we think we deserve, we are to rejoice over every sinner who comes to repentance.

The Pharisee Within

It is a sin to despise one's neighbor, but blessed is the one who is kind to the needy. Proverbs 14:21

Let's be honest, we are all a bit like the Pharisees. Who am I willing to be seen with? To whom am I willing to extend a helping hand? Who do I allow into my life? Don't we also want to be associated with people who won't embarrass us? And aren't we also sometimes only willing to help the people who are more like us?

But what if you turn the tables? What if you're the one looking for a place at someone's table? How would you feel if you were rejected because you were crippled, blind, lame or cursed? Still there is a place for you at Jesus' table.

Can you see that you should not judge and despise your fellow men? Because you are the cursed one and Jesus still invites you to His table.

Prepare a place at your table today for someone and accept them with Jesus' love.

A Welcome Guest

"Take and eat; this is My body ... This is My blood, which is poured out for many for the forgiveness of sins." Matthew 26:26, 28

What happened to the Communion table? Today it's more about who's included and who's excluded from the table. Think about it, if you're not a church member you can't eat here. If you haven't made arrangements and completed the paperwork, you're not allowed. This table is reserved for some people. And then we moan about the type of bread used, sour bread, unleavened bread, small pieces, big pieces. Not to mention the wine. Is it grape juice or not, alcohol or non-alcoholic, a silver cup, gold cup, one or two, small cups, big cups. We've locked away the beauty of God.

Jesus' message is: Open your heart to all people. Open up the table settings of your life and say, "I've once been invited while still being a sinner to the most wonderful feast, and now I want to invite others." That's the message. "I can take my seat and enjoy the feast, because my sins are forgiven, I am a welcomed guest, a guest of honor."

Christian Unity

I appeal to you, brothers and sisters, in the name of our Lord Jesus Christ, that all of you agree with one another in what you say and that there be no divisions among you, but that you be perfectly united in mind and thought. 1 Corinthians 1:10

We are quick to exclude people these days. We make up excuses of why we exclude some people: they are too old, too frivolous, too young, not educated enough, you name it. Then there's of course another big reason: they believe different things. We've made religion inaccessible. You first have to fit certain requirements, then you'll be good enough.

But it's not about our rules and regulations. It's about Jesus and Jesus only. When you were baptized, who did you choose? Jesus. It's not about theology, different denominations or Pentecost. It's about Jesus.

There won't be a bunch of separate boxes in heaven where we can go with the ones who are exactly like us. No, we're all going to the same place. And that place is with Jesus.

Accept Others

Let no debt remain outstanding, except the continuing debt to love one another, for whoever loves others has fulfilled the law. Romans 13:8

We too easily shut people out nowadays. Instead, we must open our hearts and let people in. Be honest – what does your heart look like? Who are the people present at your table? Who do you include and exclude? And why? Haven't we received the command to love the whole world?

We exclude some people, some sinners, dirty people, crippled and lame people, certain cultures and races, homosexuals. We exclude because some things don't fit into our world.

Jesus says we must invite these people into our lives and love them like He loves them. He makes it clear that although we don't accept sin, we must still love others. Jesus wants us to show them His love.

The Triune God

For there are three that testify:
the Spirit, the water and the blood; and
the three are in agreement. 1 John 5:7-8

The Trinity is God the Father, Jesus Christ and the Holy Spirit. This unity, this relationship that is at work here, is the most complete love we can ever imagine. There is no jealousy, competition, hurt; no one being offended; and nothing about own needs not being fulfilled. There is nothing like that.

In a relationship with the Trinity there is complete unanimity, and there is no petty fighting, which so often defines our "normal" earthly relationships.

This is a relationship that each of us desire to have. It is the kind of relationship where you can be yourself and love unconditionally, where your needs are met and you are not judged – a place where you can just be happy.

A relationship with the Trinity is just like this: God the Father, Jesus Christ and the Holy Spirit in complete unity.

Not Good to Be Alone

The LORD God said, "It is not good for the man to be alone. I will make a helper suitable for him." Genesis 2:18

Everything in creation was good. We read that after every day of creation, God said that it was good. But after He created man, He said that it was not good that the man was alone. He was going to make a helper suitable for him.

So even in this very first relationship, this perfect godly relationship that consists of only man and God, God said that it was not good for the man to be alone. Then the picture changed. These two people were supposed to love each other, they had to share the same companionship and camaraderie that God and man shared. God said that the man and woman should help each other. Help with what? They must help each other understand love; to experience the godliness within them; to help each other to fulfill their purpose in life.

And when two people support each other in this way, they've truly reached God's goal with marriage.

Your Partner's Helper

When the woman saw that the fruit of the tree was good for food and pleasing to the eye, and also desirable for gaining wisdom, she took some and ate it. She also gave some to her husband, who was with her, and he ate it. Genesis 3:6

Let's discuss Adam and Eve, and marriage. Did Eve help Adam? My opinion? From the frying pan into the fire. Where God said that it was not good for man to be alone and that He will make someone to help him, the exact opposite happened. Eve succumbed to the temptation of the snake, and ate the fruit. She took her husband with her and the two of them fought. They did not help each other and the ideal partnership of love was broken.

Marriage is supposed to be a place where we are equals and where we get to know the Deity, a place of loving unconditionally and being loved in return. It is supposed to be heaven on earth. Unfortunately, marriage is the complete opposite for some people. Dedicate your marriage anew to God today if you feel that you have lost your way in your marriage.

The Purpose of Marriage

He who finds a wife finds what is good and receives favor from the LORD. Proverbs 18:22

Because marriage is such an important relationship in society, we're going to discuss it a bit more. What exactly is the purpose of marriage? Why did the Lord ordain marriage? As we've established, marriage is a place of giving and receiving love, and growing in God's image.

It's important to remember that your partner is not there to make you happy. It's not his or her sole responsibility to fulfill all your selfish and uncertain needs. Your spouse is also not there to sense when something is wrong and miraculously fix it. Spouses must support each other, and help each other grow. And they must grow together in their relationship so that they can serve God better.

Only when a husband and wife stand in unity before God can they whole-heartedly serve Him, and can marriage become what God initially intended it to be.

Never Stop Growing

Grow in the grace and knowledge of our Lord and Savior Jesus Christ. To Him be glory both now and forever! 2 Peter 3:18

Let's talk about growth. How do you grow in life? When you grow in your knowledge of God, you will grow in self-discovery. God reveals Himself to you and when you learn about God, you automatically start learning more about yourself. You can therefore not discover something about God without discovering something about yourself.

The growth that takes place in your life is a godly revelation and also a "me-revelation." The more you grow in God, the more you grow in yourself. Let's look at a practical example: I learn about God, I read my Bible and I see how loving God is. The more I see Him as loving, the more I'm going to see my own lovelessness. The more I compare myself to what He did, the more I learn to see when I'm not being loving or forgiving. Are you getting to know yourself better as you grow in God?

Who Am I in Jesus?

When Jesus came to the region of Caesarea Philippi, He asked His disciples, "Who do people say the Son of Man is?" Matthew 16:13

In the New Testament Jesus asks, "Who am I?" Peter has a revelation of who Christ is, and during this revelation discovers who he himself is. Peter says to Jesus, "You are the Messiah, the Son of the living God" (Matthew 16:16).

Jesus replies, "Blessed are you, Simon son of Jonah, for this was not revealed to you by flesh and blood, but by My Father in heaven. And I tell you that you are Peter, and on this rock I will build My church, and the gates of Hades will not overcome it. I will give you the keys of the kingdom of heaven; whatever you bind on earth will be bound in heaven, and whatever you loose on earth will be loosed in heaven" (Matthew 16:17-19).

Something happens here – the better Peter gets to know Jesus, the better he gets to know himself.

A Journey of Discovery

Therefore let us move beyond the elementary teachings about Christ and be taken forward to maturity. Hebrews 6:1

Many people stop growing in life because they don't persevere in their relationship with Jesus. They are just not willing to learn from God and the Bible. They go to church, and listen to one or two interesting things, but that's it.

To grow means to go on a journey of discovery every week to get to know God better. If you don't get to know God, you won't get to know yourself. When you don't know God, you don't learn about your issues. That's why you grow when you're in a relationship with God. Let me tell you, this is the best thing that can happen to a person.

When the Lord meets you in your quiet time and talks to you, you'll learn something about God's love and mercy. And bit by bit God will help you to sort out all your issues.

Growing through Marriage

Christ is the one we proclaim, admonishing and teaching everyone with all wisdom, so that we may present everyone fully mature in Christ. Colossians 1:28

The same relationship also takes place between you and your spouse. Just like I get to know my spouse better – and in the same way I get to know God better – I discover something about myself, and grow. If there's no discovery of new things about my spouse and no growth between us, there will also be no self-discovery. It's important to remember that God must be at the center as you and your spouse discover new things about each other, as well as about yourselves.

Even conflict, unhappiness or sadness can grow a marriage. Maybe God put things together for a specific reason. God gives you a mirror that reflects your faults and shortcomings. He gives you a spouse – your mirror – to help you. Are you thankful that you're able to grow in your marriage, or do you blame your spouse because you see your own faults reflected in the mirror?

Get Rid of Your Baggage

"Do not condemn, and you will not be condemned. Forgive, and you will be forgiven." Luke 6:37

It can easily happen that we don't recognize God's helpers in our lives. Sometimes these people are a source of irritation, and as a result we don't experience the growth we were supposed to. It can also happen that people deliberately hurt us and steal our joy. However it happens, there are things in life that hurt us, and some of these hurts we carry with us for years. Something that was supposed to help us grow ends up hurting us and having a negative impact on our lives.

Sometimes the only thing we need to do is to let go. Nowhere do we find the promise that life is going to be a fairytale. It's a man-made and worldly idea that we'll only experience joy and never adversity. Is it not time to forgive those who have trespassed against us? This should be whether they did it intentionally or weren't even aware that they were stealing our joy. Set them free and forgive them and receive God's peace and joy.

Don't Sweat the Small Stuff

A heart at peace gives life to the body,
but envy rots the bones. Proverbs 14:30

What irritates you most about people? When do your loved ones touch a nerve? Have you ever ruined a good friendship or relationship because of something silly?

If you have a close relationship with someone, there will be things that bother you. People are different and what is acceptable and enjoyable for one person can be completely unacceptable to someone else.

Do you think that God might have put these people in your life to teach you patience? Perhaps you must learn to be more tolerant. And if you've given up hope already, it might be time to go back and fix things. We can't let the small things, the insignificant things, destroy our relationships.

Be calm, relax, read your Bible, pray to God and ask Him to help you be more patient with others. Remember, you might also be doing things that annoy other people.

MAY

Let Go of Your Anger

Refrain from anger and turn from wrath;
do not fret – it leads only to evil. Psalm 37:8

How is your spiritual heart? Is your heart sensitive to the will of the Lord; can your heart hear the Lord's voice; can your heart still feel the love of God? There are many things that can clog our spiritual arteries and make our hearts numb to the things of the Lord.

One of the things that narrow our spiritual arteries is anger, when we're constantly mad and want to fight about everything. Still the psalmist says we must refrain from anger because it only leads to wrath. It is better to just let some things in life go. If someone pushes in front of you in a queue, it's not worth it to still bicker about it fifteen minutes later. The person has long forgotten what they have done; you're only spoiling the mood for yourself.

Let go of your anger and give it to God. Open up your spiritual arteries and experience God's peace. You'll see for yourself that it's much better than constant fighting.

Feelings of Discontent

Keep your lives free from the love of money and be content with what you have, because God has said, "Never will I leave you; never will I forsake you." Hebrews 13:5

Feelings of discontent are not necessarily only about money. One can often feel angry about things that may or may not have happened in your life. It can also be true that people are unhappy about what others have that they don't have.

What is the result of living with a heart filled with discontent? One effect is that you become so blinded by all the things that others have that you're ungrateful for all the gifts and privileges that you've received. Discontentment creates bitterness that results in you not granting anything to anyone else. It is not pleasurable to be around discontented people, so protect your heart against it every day. Tell yourself that there will always be people who'll have more things, drive a newer car, and do more exciting things. Accept this as part of life, but also gratefully accept the abundant blessings you receive from the Lord.

Protect Your Heart

Above all else, guard your heart, for everything you do flows from it. Proverbs 4:23

"The mouth speaks what the heart is full of" (Luke 6:45). This is so true. Proverbs also says that everything you do flows from your heart.

If your heart is filled with love, joy, patience, peace and forbearance, your actions will prove it. Other people will say of such a person that he or she is beautiful on the inside. Such beauty becomes visible on your face. The opposite is also true. If your heart is filled with jealousy, unhappiness, greed, hatred and anger, it will show in your actions. You will become an unlikable person.

Guard your heart. Focus on the things that are pure and good in life. Make an effort to see the good in things. If you're battling to do this, ask the Lord to help you every day.

Strive to be a person whose beautiful heart reflects in your face.

The Heart and Mouth

It is with your heart that you believe and are justified, and it is with your mouth that you profess your faith and are saved. Romans 10:10

Listen carefully to what Paul says here: What you believe in your heart, you declare with your mouth. Where is faith found? In your heart. That's where it all starts, that's where your contact with the Lord lies.

That is also where the problem lies: in your heart. You can't claim that your heart is filled with love for God, but at the same time you harbor jealousy, envy, hatred and evil things in your heart and thoughts. There is no space in your heart for both God *and* hatred.

We often say that a specific person has a strong faith. But what does that mean? That person has a clean and strong heart. There is only space for faith in such a person's heart. Such a heart believes God is with them, such a heart grants good things to others, and such a heart is thankful for what they have received. Such a heart belongs to a child of God.

Change Your Heart

I seek You with all my heart; do not let me stray from Your commands. Psalm 119:10

Why do we sometimes feel that the faith in our hearts doesn't reach the rest of our bodies? Faith, the Word, Scripture, songs that we sing, prayers, quiet time … they don't reach our body. It's not evident in our daily tasks, in our words, and in our actions. Why not?

Because our heart is often filled with many evil things. People want to do as they please and don't realize that disobedience to God blocks the good works in their life.

What they don't realize is that doing the will of God is pleasant. It will be much more enjoyable to live a life of honesty, without corruption and lies and hypocrisy.

Obey God with your whole heart and experience the positive influence on your life.

Don't Be Afraid

The LORD is with me; I will not be afraid. What can mere mortals do to me? The LORD is with me; He is my helper. I look in triumph on my enemies. Psalm 118:6-7

People living in fear can't make good decisions. It's impossible for them to risk anything and experience anything that is wonderful. Fear can literally paralyze you so that you can't even leave your own home.

Some of the great heroes in the Bible were not without fear, but they gave their fears to God and faced them with Him. Fear is a very strong human emotion, and nobody is saying that you are never allowed to feel afraid.

Fear can save your life in some cases, or prevent you from doing something stupid. But when fear takes over your life in such a way that you can't function properly, it's time to go to God. Tell Him what you're afraid of and ask Him to free you from any irrational fear. Then you'll be free to enjoy the good things in life – even though you might be scared at first.

Don't Compare Yourself

For where you have envy and selfish ambition, there you find disorder and every evil practice. James 3:16

I think everybody has compared themselves to someone else at one stage or another. It's human nature. Phrases like "I wish I had", "If only I was", or "I want that", "If it were my money", or "If it were my job" … we've all said them.

John, Peter and the rest were disciples, but if you read the Gospels you'll find that these guys bickered from morning till noon. Who'll be number one, who is number two, who is number three? Which disciples are "in" with Jesus? Remember, they thought about an earthly kingdom and they had a plan: Jesus would sit at number one. And who'll be number two between Peter and John?

Just because Peter and John's comparison game looks more spiritual as, for instance, wanting a new car, it still doesn't make it right. In God's eyes we are all equal and perfect. We must stop desiring more.

Your Own Assignment

Jesus answered, "If I want him to remain alive until I return, what is that to you? You must follow Me." John 21:22

What Jesus was actually saying to Peter was this: "Peter, I have an assignment for you, so listen, because I have a purpose for your life." Even when the Lord is clear about what He is planning for our lives, we still wonder. We just don't want other people's life purpose to be better than our own.

The Lord says, "I have a purpose for you on earth, and it's between you and Me. I've created you in a certain way. Yes, you have a short fuse, you are impulsive, you do things before thinking, you're shy, you're withdrawn, but it's fine. That's why I want you."

God wants us to do our work with the same characteristics He created us with. Forget about the plans He has for others. Focus on His plan for you, and know that He specially selected you.

Get Out of the Way

Jesus turned and said to Peter, "Get behind Me, Satan! You are a stumbling block to Me; you do not have in mind the concerns of God, but merely human concerns." Matthew 16:23

Peter is comparing again, that's why he thinks it's the right thing to say that God will prevent Jesus from dying. And if you're comparing yourself all the time to others, Jesus will say something unusual or even shocking to you.

He'll want to get your attention and say, "It's all about you and Me. I chose you and I have a purpose for your life. Forget about other people, because this is your time, your place."

Are you a fan or a follower of Jesus? That's what Jesus is trying to tell Peter: "Be a follower, walk with Me, and follow Me." The problem is that if you compare, you'll follow the wrong people. Follow Jesus and accept His plan for your life.

Whom Do You Follow?

You, however, know all about my teaching,
my way of life, my purpose, faith,
patience, love, endurance. 2 Timothy 3:10

Silly question: Whom do you follow? TV programs, reality shows, celebrities? Or do you follow sincere men and women of God? It's important to know whom you follow, because when you admire someone you'll want to be like them.

You can admire someone for one of two reasons: either their lives look much more appealing than yours and you want what they have, or they radiate true joy and peace from God.

Sometimes you change without realizing it; therefore it's very important to follow the right people. If you believe in your heart that God has made you wonderful, you won't long for more. It won't be necessary then to follow celebrities. Keep your eyes on Jesus. And if you want to follow earthly people, follow those who are true followers of His.

Never allow your admiration for someone to steal your joy.

The Gifts You Receive

Every good and perfect gift is from above, coming down from the Father of the heavenly lights. James 1:17

Are you sometimes tempted to think that it's always other people who receive good and perfect gifts from God? You can't be more wrong; it is *you* who receives good gifts from God's hand.

God hasn't changed, and what we read in the Bible is still true. If we read that God gives good and perfect gifts, why do we doubt? Is it because we don't get everything we want? It so often happens that God gives us wonderful things, but we don't even see it because we would rather have what someone else has.

God knows us and He knows what we need. God knows what we can handle and what we can't; therefore He gives us exactly what is right. Open your hands today and thankfully receive the gifts that He wants to give to you, and only you.

Don't Be Stingy

May your hearts be fully committed to the LORD our God, to live by His decrees and obey His commands, as at this time. 1 Kings 8:61

To a heart that is never content or satisfied, nothing will ever be good enough; such a heart is always scared of missing out. A discontented heart is stingy.

Why are discontented hearts so tightfisted? Because they compare what they have to others, and then they want more than others. But here's the surprise: There will always be someone who will have more than you, who is prettier than you, cleverer than you. Stop comparing, because it makes you stingy.

Let's define stinginess: It means you're too scared to live. It means you're not living in every moment. It has nothing to do with money. It means you have love, but you're not living out your love because you're protecting it. The way to multiply love is to share it. The way to increase your gifts and talents is by giving. That's how God operates. The more you give, the more you receive.

Shout for Joy!

So rejoice in the Lord and be glad, all you who obey Him! Shout for joy, all you whose hearts are pure!

Psalm 32:11

God wants His people to be joyful. In Nehemiah 8:10 the Lord says, "The joy of the Lord is your strength."

The Lord wants His people to be happy, because someone who has a joyful heart doesn't have time to compare themselves to others – they only enjoy life.

In the Psalms, David writes that we must rejoice and be glad. Are you a joyful person? Make an effort today to see the joyous side of life, and find something to smile about.

Even better, see what you can do to make someone else smile.

Laughter Is Good Medicine

Our mouths were filled with laughter, our tongues with songs of joy. Then it was said among the nations, "The Lord has done great things for them." The Lord has done great things for us, and we are filled with joy.

Psalm 126:2

Laughter is not evil. In fact, it is good for our health. Unfortunately, as adults we don't laugh enough.

I've read recently that children under the age of six laugh 125 times a day. From seven years and up, the average person laughs only 15 times a day.

Don't be like the Pharisees who condemned people because they were joyful. We must all laugh more, because the joy of the Lord keeps your heart in good condition.

When we think of all the blessings we have in Christ, we can't help but rejoice!

A Cheerful Heart

The cheerful heart has a
continual feast. Proverbs 15:15

It is a choice whether to enjoy life or not. And you're allowed to enjoy life. Are you going to start being thankful for what you've received in life? Are you going to tell yourself, "This is my life and I'm going to enjoy it, because I'm also anointed with the oil of joyfulness in Christ"?

Proverbs 17:22 says that, "A joyful heart is good medicine" and it has been scientifically proven that laughter is good for you so make a conscious effort to see the less serious side of life. Get excited about life, and about the work that the Lord is doing in and around you.

Laugh at yourself. Laugh, because it's good for your heart. Enjoy the life that God has given you.

A Heart Condition

As water reflects the face, so one's life reflects the heart. Proverbs 27:19

We have many problems in our country today – politics, economic growth, crime, you name it. And we can talk about these problems at length. It is sometimes the only things people talk about. I, however, believe that the biggest problem is the condition of our heart.

I see the symptoms of spiritual heart disease everywhere I go. We sit with spiritual cholesterol that affects our whole lives. Why? We focus on the bad things, the things we don't like, and later they become all we see. The more we focus on the bad, the fewer good things we see.

Open your heart – and eyes – to the good things. See the blessings from the Father's hand. You don't have to die of spiritual heart failure; things *can* be different.

Guard Your Heart

The peace of God, which transcends all understanding, will guard your hearts and your minds in Christ Jesus. Philippians 4:6-7

Guard your heart. How much money do you spend on safeguarding your house? Do you have an alarm system and electric fence around your house? We can keep going and discover that people spend a lot of money to secure their homes. Do you have medical insurance, and are you someone who spends extra money each month saving for their children or even for themselves?

How much do we spend on guarding our spiritual hearts? Most of the time the answer is not a lot. Some of us buy a spiritual book or CD or sermon to get spiritual food, but it's not close to what we spend on protecting and guarding the physical things in our lives. Think about it. Physical things are here today and gone tomorrow. Jesus says, "Do not store up for yourselves treasures on earth" (Matthew 6:19). Nobody is saying that you can't buy things for yourself, but is it not equally important to invest in eternal things?

How to Guard Your Heart

Create in me a pure heart, O God, and renew a steadfast spirit within me. Psalm 51:10

The next question is: How do I guard my heart? Jesus said that you live from your heart, and speak from your heart, and we know that "the mouth speaks what the heart is full of" (Luke 6:45). It is your life, your heart is your life. We can elaborate on it with many Scriptures, but only one scenario: your heart is the place where God dwells.

We should be sensitive to God's voice, but we're too busy and rushed. That's a heart problem, because your heart tells you whether it's going well between you and God. Your heart tells you that the Lord is with you, and in you if He is satisfied and if everything is fine. It's your heart that becomes numb, cold and singed, and all of a sudden you merely exist. You just go through the motions and miss the small still voice of the Lord. You miss the love, the vision, the calling. It's in your heart that these things happen. We must help each other every day to keep our hearts healthy.

VIPs and VDPs

But thanks be to God, who always leads us as captives in Christ's triumphal procession and uses us to spread the aroma of the knowledge of Him everywhere. 2 Corinthians 2:14

There are two types of people in life: The VIPs (very important people), full of positive energy and spreading joy wherever they go, and the VDPs (very draining people). These people literally drain every bit of joy from your life.

Because we are exposed to all kinds of people on a daily basis, it's not really possible to avoid them. The VDPs often cause pain, hurt, guilt, fear and more. They focus on the negative things and don't grant anyone any happiness. We must carefully watch out so that these people do not steal our joy. Whether the people around you have a pleasant aroma or are draining your energy, it is your responsibility how you're going to react. Choose to see the good things and disregard the negative things. Watch out that you don't also become a VDP, but rather someone who shares joy and peace.

The Dangers of Stress

Cast your cares on the LORD and He will sustain you;
He will never let the righteous be shaken. Psalm 55:22

Our lives are busy. There's a constant flurry in our hearts, a continuous feeling of discontent, an ongoing competition with ourselves and others. We *must* win.

This must-win syndrome is born from thoughts that God is not in control anymore. Such people believe they are responsible for their own survival. Other people think worrying is part of who they are – it's in their genes; they are powerless against it.

Is it not time to change our image of God? God wants to and will care for us. He is after all our Father. It's not always easy, but give your cares to Him. You can know this truth: He will never let you down. Whatever the reason for your constant worry and stress, give your cares to Him, and ask for His peace within your soul. He won't disappoint you.

Trust in God

He will be the sure foundation
for your times. Isaiah 33:6

One often hears someone say that they don't easily trust people. You've perhaps said it yourself. We've all been hurt or betrayed by someone we thought we could trust. No one is exempt from such pain. What is important is how we react toward such pain. We are sometimes so severely hurt that we even lose our trust in God.

Yet we read in the Bible that God is our sure foundation and that we can trust Him. Our trust in people can perhaps be tarnished, but God will never betray us or disappoint us. Don't allow your disillusionment in people to influence the rest of your life – we might become so determined to get back at the person who betrayed us that we become completely bitter.

Let go of your urge to pay back someone for what they have done. Ask the Lord to help you distinguish who you can trust, and be sure that He will never leave you in the lurch.

A Heart Filled with Anger

Now you must also rid yourselves of all such things as these: anger, rage, malice, slander, and filthy language from your lips. Colossians 3:8

Some people are always mad about everything. They are unhappy that things didn't turn out the way they wanted. They are mad at others who have more than they do. They are angry about shortcomings they see in themselves but don't want to acknowledge. They are just angry at everyone and everything. The worst is that they take this anger out on others, because they don't know how to deal with it.

The Bible is very clear on anger, and says that we must let go of it. If you're struggling with anger in your life, go to God and discuss it with Him. Ask Him to help you find the root cause and to work at it.

Let God free you from the chains of anger. It is not something you'll get right in your own strength. Work with the Lord and ask Him to take your anger away.

Don't Fear

Even though I walk through the darkest valley,
I will fear no evil, for You are with me. Psalm 23:4

We are all aware of the state that our country and the world is in. We know about violence, crime, the fear of losing your job, economic crises … we sit with a load of fear on our shoulders. The result of this fear is not living life fully; you lock yourself up, too scared to make a mistake. You're afraid to take risks, you're too scared to go out, you're afraid of being obedient to His voice.

Fear robs you of everything that life has to offer. Fear clogs our spiritual arteries and poses a huge threat to the condition of our hearts. If you know you're heading for a heart attack, you will do everything to avoid it, right? You will eat healthier, exercise more, and reduce stress. So why aren't we doing the same with our spiritual hearts? Why don't we go to God straightaway and ask Him to take our fears away?

Hearing God's Voice

Sow righteousness for yourselves, reap the fruit of unfailing love, and break up your unplowed ground; for it is time to seek the LORD, until He comes and showers His righteousness on you. Hosea 10:12

You and I have the voice of God; we are His children, we have His Spirit in us, we have His answers for a time such as this, we have it all inside us. But too many of us sit with spiritual cholesterol; therefore we can't live victorious lives. We barely survive.

God wants to work through us; He has all the answers to all our problems. But the sin in our lives prevents us from hearing His voice. We must first get rid of sin – the spiritual cholesterol that we have in our hearts. Only then will we be able to hear His voice clearly. We can experience the joy of being part of the solution that He gives us. Listen to what God wants to say to you and live according to His guidance and directives. His promises are clear: If we seek His will, He will shower His righteousness on us and our country.

Hearts Filled with Fear

"So do not fear, for I am with you; do not be dismayed, for I am your God. I will strengthen you and help you; I will uphold you with my righteous right hand. For I am the LORD your God who takes hold of your right hand and says to you, Do not fear; I will help you." Isaiah 41:10, 13

"Do not fear" – that is the message. And if there is a personal message for all people, it is "do not be afraid." In our country, we believe that you have to be vigilant and can't go through life with blinkers on.

We must sift our fears and find out which are healthy fears. Have you heard about good cholesterol? There is good cholesterol and healthy fear. There are also massive amounts of unhealthy fear and bad cholesterol; therefore you must determine which ones drive you. Nine out of ten times it's unhealthy.

A small percentage is healthy and necessary to protect yourself and your life. I don't know about you, but I hate living in fear.

Fear Leads to Death

"Have I not commanded you? Be strong and courageous. Do not be afraid; do not be discouraged, for the LORD your God will be with you wherever you go." Joshua 1:9

We've seen that healthy fear can keep one safe. The problem is that some people's fears start governing them, and as a result everything poses a threat. They are scared of everything and everyone, and later fear takes over their entire lives.

God tells us not to be afraid. We must be strong and courageous, because He is with us. He knows about our concerns for our families and loved ones.

God knows that the world out there is not a safe place. But He says that He will be with us wherever we go. Despite our fear, God is in control. He hasn't left us, and He never will.

How Do You View God?

Among the gods there is none like You,
Lord; no deeds can compare with Yours.
All the nations You have made will come and
worship before You, Lord; they will bring glory
to Your name. For You are great and do marvelous deeds; You alone are God. Psalm 86:8-10

Who or what is God to you? Is He someone who is somewhat involved in people's lives? Or did He just create man and is otherwise not interested? The way you see God influences your relationship with Him.

Let me explain: A person who claims that God is involved in people's lives is also the one who claims that He created the earth, and has been involved in the lives of people from Adam and Eve, Abraham and Moses, to this day. Such a person believes He is present and also believes when Jesus says, "I am with you always, to the very end of the age" (Matthew 28:20). This person believes that God is with them every day. Is that not the type of relationship you want with God? The alternative is an ordinary life with limited joy.

Nothing to Fear

"Do not be afraid, you who are highly esteemed," he said. "Peace! Be strong now; be strong." Daniel 10:19

If you believe God is with you every day, you won't experience overwhelming fear. If you believe that God left us here and returned to heaven, you may be left with the fear of "having to take care of everything, making sure the sun rises and the moon shines, letting it rain, ensuring the rivers flow, taking care of ..."

Let's be honest, a human being can't do this. Now we become fearful. The biggest consequence of a fearful life is disobedience. How do we link the two? Listen carefully: God asks you to do something and because of fear you don't move. You don't believe that God is in control of the situation, you're too scared to do anything because you have no guarantee that you will succeed.

But the one who knows that God is still in complete control is obedient to Him, because they know that God is with them.

Take a Chance

When you ask, you must believe and not doubt, because the one who doubts is like a wave of the sea, blown and tossed by the wind. James 1:6

We know that fear keeps us from doing great things for the Lord. A doubtful person is like the waves of the sea, blown and tossed by the wind.

God says "take a chance," but the fear inside us leads to indecisiveness. We don't want to make a mistake, because a mistake is costly and there are consequences, and people will gossip and ridicule. And because we fear, we are hesitant and can't obey the will of God. We can't expect to receive anything from the Lord, because we can't make decisions.

The Lord has dreams and plans for us, a voice that whispers, "Dare to dream, do it!" but because we're doubtful and fearful, we don't make a decision. He can thus not count on us. And therefore He is going to stop whispering to us. It is a frightening thought that God won't use us because we're too scared.

Love Drives out Fear

This is how love is made complete among us so that we will have confidence on the day of judgment: In this world we are like Jesus. 1 John 4:17

The opposite of fear is love. You know that God loves you and that He is present in your life. Do you live with confidence as you wait for Judgment Day? Are you ready to stand before Jesus and ask: "How did I do? Did I live my life fully for You? I know I've made mistakes, but I know You love and forgive me." Are you ready?

Why does John say that we don't have confidence for the Day of Judgment? Because of our fears. We haven't received His love. We are afraid. What will He say? How did I live? Listen to what He also says: "There is no fear in love. But perfect love drives out fear, because fear has to do with punishment." (1 John 4:18). Perfect love has no place for fear. Perfect love drives out fear, because fear is obsessed with punishment, and whoever keeps on being fearful hasn't mastered perfect love. What is perfect love? God is with me, and He loves me and He has a dream for my life.

God Is with You

"The LORD bless you and keep you; the LORD make His face shine on you and be gracious to you; the LORD turn His face toward you and give you peace." Numbers 6:24-26

God is always available. We don't have to be afraid because God loves us and is always with us. Don't be afraid; God is always available when we need Him.

Numbers 6 is a promise from the Lord for each one of us. We must apply this prayer to our lives. If you make this prayer your own on a daily basis, God will be with you. He will hear your prayers. He will care for you.

Meditate on this prayer whenever you can. Believe the promise that He is with you and that He loves you. Make this promise your own and in this way become free from fear, uncertainty and doubt. Strive for a healthy spiritual heart and make His promises your own.

JUNE

How Do Others See You?

Whoever claims to live in Him
must live as Jesus did. 1 John 2:6

How would you like others to remember you? What do people say about you? Remember, people gossip in any case. When your family holiday is over and you drive away, the rest of the family talk about you. They talk about you and your sweet children. Or maybe they're glad you've left.

The question is not whether they're going to talk about you, but what you want them to say about you. Are they going to say you're just an ordinary person like all the others? Or do you want them to say something like: You are extraordinary. Wow, you are someone special. You're just put together differently.

What do you want others to say about you? We all want them to say, "What a really nice person!" Or more than that: Do you want them to see Jesus in your actions?

Are You Extraordinary?

Until we all reach unity in the faith and in the knowledge of the Son of God and become mature, attaining to the whole measure of the fullness of Christ. Ephesians 4:13

Let's talk about the word *extraordinary*. We all know people who are extraordinary in something; in other words, an extraordinary athlete, business person, artist or musician.

I'm not referring to being extraordinary in your work or the likes; I'm talking about being an extraordinary *person*: extraordinary in your faith in God. It's different, because an extraordinary person does things differently, lives differently and talks differently – their whole life is just different. Don't allow sin and our modern-day culture to make you less extraordinary. Society wants us to "be ordinary." People will make you feel as if you're setting the standards too high. Don't let their satisfaction with being ordinary rob you of a life that can be extraordinary. Don't become complacent and accept your lot until you've become what God made you to be!

The Same as Everyone Else

Samson answered her, "If anyone ties me with seven fresh bowstrings that have not been dried, I'll become as weak as any other man." Judges 16:7

We all know the story of Samson and Delilah and how Delilah nagged Samson to tell her the source of his strength. In Samson's own words, "I'll become as weak as any other man," we clearly see what sin does. It makes you ordinary, exactly the same as everyone else.

Do you know that when we are tied up with ropes – when culture ties us up, when friends or our social group ties us up, when the guys at work tie us up – we become like all the other ordinary people.

Have you been saved by God? Is the same Spirit that was in Jesus also in you? To just be ordinary? No, no, no. What does the Spirit do to us who believe in the blood of Jesus and the gospel? It is supposed to make us extraordinary. It is supposed to make us somebody unique – to be different in every way.

For Such a Time as This

In those days Israel had no king;
everyone did as they saw fit. Judges 21:25

There is something extraordinary inside you and me: the Spirit of God. We live in a country with a unique political composition, a unique economy, a country that is one of a kind, and we have the extraordinary Spirit in us to enable us to make an extraordinary difference.

I want to link our time with the time of the judges. The judges determined what was right and wrong. After Moses and Joshua died, the people were without a leader and started to sin. The reason is because as soon as there is no leader, everyone becomes just ordinary citizens. Everything is OK, nothing is right or wrong, everyone does as they please.

This what being extraordinary is all about: stepping away from the idea of doing what you want when you want, and with whom you want. Extraordinary means stepping up to what is right and doing it – even if you're the only one.

Light Bearers in a Dark World

Do everything without grumbling or arguing, so that you may become blameless and pure, "children of God without fault in a warped and crooked generation." Philippians 2:14-15

You can see – without being overly pessimistic – all the things that are wrong in the world today. To a great extent, people are doing what they please. Many people feel "everyone" is doing it, so it's easy to go with the flow and get involved in acts of darkness.

But that's not what God has called us for. We might live in a dark world, but He wants us to shine bright, like stars in the sky, by living meticulously according to the message that leads to life. God calls us today to be extraordinary stars, stars who shine while everyone else is corrupt and dishonest, negative and deceitful. In a time where everyone is pessimistic, you can be extraordinary. You can have extraordinary faith that declares that God is going to do something great in the world.

How Do You Want to Live?

Then you will shine among them like stars in the sky as you hold firmly to the word of life. Philippians 2:15-16

Most people would like to be extraordinary. An extraordinary spouse, an extraordinary parent to your children, an exceptional worker and child of God. I want to do it, I want to live it. But how? How can I become extraordinary?

Not only is it a choice to live an extraordinary life, but it is also a biblical command. How will people see that we are living extraordinary lives? By being bearers of light, carrying the gospel to others.

Do you want to live extraordinarily? Yes. Do you want to serve God? Yes. Do you want people to turn back to God? Yes, I want to see people serving the Lord again. How am I going to do this? By living close to God and doing only what He asks of me, whether it's difficult or easy.

Becoming Brave

The angel of the LORD came and sat down under the oak in Ophrah that belonged to Joash the Abiezrite, where his son Gideon was threshing wheat in a winepress to keep it from the Midianites. Judges 6:11

A wine press wasn't usually located in the sun because the wine fermented too quickly. One usually threshed wheat outside where it was windy, but Gideon did it inside the press because he was afraid of the Midianites. Nonetheless, the angel greeted him with the following words, "The LORD is with you, mighty warrior" (Judges 6:12).

I think Gideon must have said, "No, sorry, wrong address. I mean, that can't be me, Lord. I'm hiding in the press and am struggling to thresh the wheat. I'm not a mighty warrior."

The Lord, however, doesn't see us for who we think we are, but for who He knows we can be. Never allow your own insecurities to prevent you from doing great things for the Lord. He won't use you unless He also strengthens you.

I Don't Think I Can

"Pardon me, my lord," Gideon replied, "but how can I save Israel? My clan is the weakest in Manasseh, and I am the least in my family." Judges 6:15

Gideon is not convinced that he is the right person for the work of the Lord. He carefully explains that he is in fact the weakest in his clan. He doesn't think God can use him.

Gideon knows the history of God's work. He knows of God's mighty works and how He freed the Israelites from Egypt. But Gideon believed God abandoned them and gave them over to the Midianite army. Gideon is so disappointed that he doesn't believe God has the power to save them. And because he doesn't believe in God's power, he can't imagine how he can make a difference. He is unaware of his own strength in the Lord.

Aren't we also like that? We get so blinded by other people's disobedience that we completely forget about God's omnipotence. Stop looking at yourself as the weakest link and rather see yourself as God's mighty warrior.

The Faith Struggle

Then Gideon said to God, "Do not be angry with me. Let me make just one more request. Allow me one more test." Judges 6:39

How do you become extraordinary? You start seeing a different picture of yourself; in fact, you see God's picture of yourself. You see what God sees and He sees an extraordinary person. God sees extraordinary potential, He sees that you have strength and spirit and something special, and you can do something. He sees you differently.

Gideon says, "No, not me. You're making a mistake, Lord." And despite God's signs, Gideon still doubts. Many of us also first ask for a sign before we do something for the Lord. You want an extraordinary marriage, to be an extraordinary parent and an extraordinary witness at your workplace, and so want to have extraordinary faith. But you still ask for a sign that God is really speaking to you. We are scared of making a mistake, but while we are scared, we can only just stay ordinary. Extraordinary people trust in God and do what He asks without hesitation.

We Are God's Children

Dear friends, now we are children of God, and what we will be has not yet been made known. But we know that when Christ appears, we shall be like Him, for we shall see Him as He is. 1 John 3:2

We have a habit at our church of appointing people who need "tuning down," rather than selecting someone who needs to be livened up. It's more difficult to try and blow some life into someone than to tell them, "Slow down. I like your energy, but let's channel it in the right direction." And that is what the Lord is saying to you today. How do you see yourself? Dull? Average? Or do you hear the Spirit of the Lord saying that you are extraordinary, that the Spirit is in you and you are His child?

Do you see Jesus as ordinary? Or do you see Him as extraordinary? He was someone who listened to the Father and changed the world.

I see Jesus as absolutely extraordinary. I see Jesus as a love I can't contain. I see my Jesus as holy and as a life I dream of living. How do *you* see Jesus?

Strong in God

The LORD answered, "I will be with you." Judges 6:16

St. Augustine said that when we get to heaven one day we won't sin anymore, not because we can't sin, but because we won't want to, since we will have seen Him. How do you see yourself? A more important question is rather how you can change the way you see yourself. There are two vital aspects: to believe what God says about you and to attempt great things for Him.

The Scripture verse above says something wonderful: "I will be with you." After all Gideon's excuses, God says this one thing to him – "I will be with you." That changes everything.

If you believe He is with you, you'll handle situations differently, because you'll know that the God of the universe, the Creator, is with you. What a wonderful thought! God is with me, and therefore I am strong no matter what.

We Are Never Alone

"And surely I am with you always, to the very end of the age." Matthew 28:20

These are Jesus' last words before His Ascension: "I am with you." We can start living extraordinary lives if we believe and take a chance.

I know of someone in our church who was like Gideon. In her own eyes she was unimportant. She was lonely and decided to make friends online. She built a friendship with a man in Scotland who had cancer. He wasn't a religious person, but one day she just decided to pray for him. Not long afterward, he sent her a message saying that he needed to find God. She led him to faith online and he met the Lord.

Listen carefully: It takes an ordinary person who starts living boldly. My question to you is this: Are you extraordinary or plain? Are you going to listen to the promptings of the Lord when He asks you to go and make a difference for Him?

Holy in the Lord

"'Consecrate yourselves and be holy, because I am the LORD your God. Keep My decrees and follow them. I am the LORD, who makes you holy." Leviticus 20:7-8

What are your first thoughts when you hear the words "be extraordinary"? For me these words are very appealing; they attract me because I want to be extraordinary. I want to stand out in every area of my life – I want to make a difference, I want to be used by the Lord and I want to be an instrument in His hand.

The words "be extraordinary" are therefore words I run toward, saying, "Lord, help me to be extraordinary." We have the perfect example in Jesus of an extraordinary life. God also says in the Old Testament that we must obey His commands and decrees and live accordingly. When we do this whole-heartedly, we are extraordinary people in the Lord. If we really want to stand out in every area of our lives, and make a difference by serving Him, we must dedicate ourselves to Him and live holy lives. Dedicate your life anew to Him today.

Say No to Sinful Desires

Better what the eye sees than the roving of the appetite. This too is meaningless, a chasing after the wind. Ecclesiastes 6:9

How can we live for God amidst our dark desires? "Dark desires" sounds very heavy, right? And no, it's not your craving for dark chocolate.

This subject is very relevant. We are confronted by our desires every day. Nobody is exempt from it. Our whole lives are filled with desires, but how we react to them is an indication of our relationship with the Lord. The Lord created us to want things. Desires for clothes, cars, money, jewelry.

Then there are also desires to do good things – at work, in our careers, our studies, our sport. The problem, however, steps in when we desire things we shouldn't. No one is saying that you shouldn't improve, but watch out that material things don't start dominating your life.

The Desires of the Flesh

"Watch and pray so that you will not fall into temptation. The spirit is willing, but the flesh is weak." Matthew 26:41

Along with our desires for material possessions, we were also created with a desire to live in contact with others. We have a desire for intimacy.

In its most basic form, it is the desire not to be alone. We want to have a relationship with others and experience things together. Then there is of course the desire for sexual things. There's nothing wrong with this; after all, this is how God created us. But because we live after the Fall, these things aren't always innocent. Sexual desire inside a marriage is good. That is, however, where it must stop – the Bible is clear about this: You shall not covet your neighbor's wife. Or your neighbor's husband.

If you are struggling with such desires, go to God. Lay them before Him and ask Him to free you of them. It's not worth it to risk destroying your life over momentary pleasure.

The Desire to Follow Jesus

When he saw Jesus passing by, he said, "Look, the Lamb of God!" When the two disciples heard Him say this, they followed Jesus. Turning around, Jesus saw them following and asked, "What do you want?" They said, "Rabbi" (which means "Teacher"), "where are You staying?" John 1:36-38

Let's focus a bit more on desires that are good. We read in John how two of Jesus' disciples heard John say that Jesus is the Lamb of God. They followed Him then and there. Jesus turned around and saw that they were following Him and asked, "What do you want?"

It's a question of desire, because we read in Philippians 4:6, "Do not be anxious about anything, but in every situation, by prayer and petition, with thanksgiving, present your requests to God."

He wants to hear the longings of your heart. He wants to work with you in terms of your desires. These desires must of course be after Him. They must be a longing to know Him better and to do more for His kingdom. For that He will never turn you down.

Twisted Desires

Each person is tempted when they are dragged away by their own evil desire and enticed. Then, after desire has conceived, it gives birth to sin; and sin, when it is full-grown, gives birth to death. James 1:14-15

We know that our desires can become crooked, twisted and clouded. Let me give you a good example: A good desire is to say, "I hope my team wins every game this season." A twisted desire is to wish that a team loses every game. Something that starts out as a good desire can easily become distorted because of our sinful nature.

Suppose two people meet at work. They like each other and work together well. Both are married, but not to each other. Before long, their relationship could turn into a dark desire. Before they realize it, they may cross a line.

Are you in a similar situation? Do you perhaps welcome attention that you know is wrong? End the friendship and ask God to help you stand strong against temptation.

God Is a Merciful God

I am convinced that neither death nor life, neither angels nor demons, neither the present nor the future, nor any powers, neither height nor depth, nor anything else in all creation, will be able to separate us from the love of God that is in Christ Jesus our Lord. Romans 8:38-39

If you say, "I know what it feels like to walk through the door of dark desires," then I'm glad. Why am I glad? Because I can assure you that Christ's love and mercy can reach the place you find yourself at. Nothing is in any case hidden from Him; just take your sins to Him and lay them at His feet.

We are all sinners, but I want to assure you that nothing can separate you from His love, and nothing will be able to separate you from His mercy. He can pull you out of any undesirable situation. He'll work with you, and if you show sincere remorse, He will forgive you and save your life. He wants to restore, He wants to heal and He wants to save people from their dark desires today.

A Lesson from Samson

The woman gave birth to a boy and named him Samson. He grew and the LORD blessed him, and the Spirit of the LORD began to stir him. Judges 13:24-25

Samson received a great promise: He was going to be the one to conquer the Philistines, and extraordinary miracles would happen through him. The Spirit of the Lord rested on him and he was abundantly blessed. We also read that Samson liked pretty girls, especially Philistine women, who were actually the enemy.

Samson put his own desires first, and it caused him great adversity. We can learn a clear lesson from Samson's life. Samson was dedicated to God from birth and saw many miracles take place. Still he yielded to the temptation of the flesh. One almost feels inclined to ask that if it happened to Samson, what hope is there for us? We must never forget to walk closely with God, and to put His will first and foremost in our lives. If you ever have doubts about something, discuss it with God. He won't let you down.

God's Plans, Not Ours

His father and mother replied, "Isn't there an acceptable woman among your relatives or among all our people? Must you go to the uncircumcised Philistines to get a wife?" But Samson said to his father, "Get her for me. She's the right one for me." Judges 14:3

Samson insisted on marrying a Philistine girl. His parents probably wanted to ask what was wrong with him for him to do such a thing. He was a Christian boy and this woman didn't even serve the Lord. What was she going to bring to the marriage? All that Samson had to say was that he liked her and they must get her for him.

Samson's parents didn't realize that this desire actually came from God. The Philistines ruled over Israel at that stage. Now this left me speechless: Even in a seemingly completely wrong decision, God used it to get to the Philistines. He wanted Samson to spy on them and destroy them. And this girl was perhaps the perfect way to do it. If some things seem inexplicable, think about the story of Samson.

The Power of God

The Spirit of the LORD came powerfully upon him so that he tore the lion apart with his bare hands as he might have torn a young goat. Judges 14:6

Samson was blessed with physical power and strength. I often wonder what Samson really looked like. I don't think the pictures in children's Bibles are accurate – Samson looks like a body builder. However, the Bible says that every time the Spirit of the Lord came over him, he was able to do these great things. I think Samson looked like any other Israelite, but when the Spirit of the Lord and the power of God came over him, he acted from that source of power.

We see people even today who don't look like they can achieve much. It might only be when they open their mouths that we realize we are in the presence of a great man or woman of God. Perhaps it was the same with Samson's strength. We are all ordinary until the power of the Lord comes over us. Then we become extraordinary in word and deed. We must therefore not judge people based on their outward appearance.

Powerless against the World

Samson's wife threw herself on him, sobbing, "You hate me! You don't really love me. You've given my people a riddle, but you haven't told me the answer." "I haven't even explained it to my father or mother," he replied, "so why should I explain it to you?" Judges 14:16

Samson gave a riddle to the guests at his feast. If they found the right answer, he would give them thirty linen garments and thirty sets of clothes. But the guests couldn't solve the riddle and they later asked Samson's wife to try and get the answer from him.

So it happened that his wife started sobbing, nagging him to give her the answer. He told her that he didn't even give the answer to his own parents. She continued nagging him, and we read in the Bible that he gave it to her because she kept bothering him. He couldn't take it anymore. This is only the secret to the riddle, but can you see how he gets lured in? It is clear that without God's strength we too are powerless against the world.

Big Sins Start Small

Catch for us the foxes, the little foxes
that ruin the vineyards. Song of Songs 2:15

The devil doesn't tell you to leave your wife, and he doesn't tell you to steal money from your work. No, that's not how it starts. He starts small. He'll say, "You can take the item – you need it and you don't have money at the moment. It's only the 23rd of the month; pay day is in two days' time. And if you get your pay, you can buy a new one and put the old one back" … or whatever the case may be.

That's why a child who tells lies is just as bad as a cheating husband or wife, or someone who steals money from their place of work. That is how the secrets start and where the cracks start showing.

We must never think that small sins are better or more acceptable than big sins. Sin is sin, and it's the little foxes that ruin the vineyard.

Dark Desires

Some time later, he fell in love with a woman in the Valley of Sorek whose name was Delilah. Judges 16:4

Delilah portrayed a desire, and in particular Samson's desire for a beautiful woman. She would become the deepest, darkest desire in his life for whom he was prepared to give up everything.

Delilah is promised eleven hundred shekels of silver if she manages to find out where Samson's strength comes from. She then asks him, "Tell me the secret of your great strength and how you can be tied up and subdued." Samson answers, "If anyone ties me with seven fresh bowstrings … I'll become as weak as any other man" (Judges 16:6-7).

Now this is what dark desires do to us: they want to tie us down. I wonder how many people today feel weighed down; how many people feel that they can't be extraordinary. They have too many secrets they would have to bring out into the open, but just as many that they still need to hide. They are tied down and overwhelmed. And that's exactly what dark desires do. Don't fall into the trap of your dark desires like Samson did.

Choosing Ordinary

Then she said to him, "How can you say, 'I love you,' when you won't confide in me? This is the third time you have made a fool of me and haven't told me the secret of your great strength." Judges 16:15

Delilah nagged Samson for days on end. With such nagging she prodded him day after day until he was sick to death of it. Then he made the biggest mistake of his life. He told her that his hair had never been cut and he had been dedicated to God from birth. "If my head were shaved, my strength would leave me, and I would become as weak as any other man" (Judges 16:17).

It shows that he was aware of his calling and the task to which the Lord had called him. Many of us have felt like that: If I walk through that door, and if I make that decision, if that feeling comes over me, I think, *But, Lord, I'm Your child, how can I talk like that and act like that, how can I make such wrong decisions? I must be out of my mind.* Can you imagine that someone would be willing to give up everything to be ordinary?

The Samson Inside

Then the Philistines seized him, gouged out his eyes and took him down to Gaza. Binding him with bronze shackles, they set him to grinding grain in the prison. Judges 16:21

We continue with Samson's story. While he was sleeping, Delilah shaved his head. The Philistines came, overpowered him and gouged out his eyes. His hair was the sign of his strength, his symbolic pact with the Lord. The Lord had told him to look after it and care for it.

We are quick to question how Samson could have been so stupid and to fall for Delilah's tricks. It was not intended for him to fall, and it was never meant to be like that. Samson was different, he was extraordinary, but he exchanged it for his deepest, darkest desires.

Don't we also do exactly that sometimes? We would give up our greatest gifts for things that are fleeting and passing. Samson found himself literally and figuratively in the dark. It became a constant reminder that he gave in to darkness. How many of us are also in the dark?

All Is Not Lost

The hair on his head began to grow again after it had been shaved. Judges 16:22

Once again the mercy of the Lord is evident. The time in prison was a time of restoration for Samson. The Lord was restoring him to his former glory. Praise the Lord for restoration, but there comes a time after sin when you need to bear the consequences, and that can leave one ordinary and powerless.

During the Philistines great celebration in honor of Dagon, they called for Samson to entertain them. He stood between two pillars, because he couldn't see, and needed to lean against them. Then He turned to God, and asked Him to strengthen him once more. "Let me with one blow get revenge on the Philistines for my two eyes" (Judges 16:28).

The Lord strengthened Samson one last time; he pushed with all his might and down came the temple. About 3,000 men and women died that day. Here we see that all is not lost if we give in to darkness. We can turn back to God at any time – He is waiting with outstretched arms.

Stand Up

As a prisoner for the Lord, then, I urge you to live a life worthy of the calling you have received. Ephesians 4:1

God calls us to be extraordinary. People like this always ask in any given situation what an extraordinary person would do. In a time where people don't respect others or the law anymore, it has become more important than ever for extraordinary people to stand up and answer God's call on their lives.

Are you brave enough to stand up for what's right among your friends or at work? Do you have the courage to raise your children according to biblical standards, or are you satisfied that they're just going with the flow? Are you daring enough to stand up for the oppressed, for those who are regarded as unimportant in people's eyes? If we can fulfill the calling we've received from God, we can look forward to a brighter and better future. Don't be afraid – God will strengthen you for the task. He will give you the strength to become a new person.

Times without Leaders

Whenever the Lord raised up a judge for them, He was with the judge and saved them out of the hands of their enemies as long as the judge lived. Judges 2:18

We live in almost the same time as that of the judges. There were no kings or anybody to tell Israel what to do and what was right or wrong. Everybody did what they wanted, just like today.

There weren't any judges to show the people the will of God. What we read in the book of Judges is that the people served the Lord, but then they started to sin and worship idols. They wanted what others had – money and pleasure. Every time they sinned, they became prisoners of other tribes. Then God established another judge, who said, "Follow me. Let's follow the Lord again," and went on to live an extraordinary life.

The Lord felt sorry for His people when they complained about their suffering. The Lord also feels sorry for us because we are without a leader. He feels sorry for us because we don't have moral values and principles and a system to tell us right from wrong.

Whom Do You Follow?

Blessed is the one who does not walk in step with the wicked or stand in the way that sinners take or sit in the company of mockers, but whose delight is in the law of the LORD. Psalm 1:1-2

Recently I was listening to the radio while driving. During a talk show, a man phoned in about a certain legislation in the country and said the following: "I don't need a country or people or a president to give me rules, I can decide for myself what is right and wrong."

It was as if his words come straight from the book of Judges. We don't listen to a president or a political leader or even to the church. Do you follow the country or the church's rules about abortion? About homosexuality? About divorce? No, I will do what is right and what the Bible teaches.

These are the times in which we live. And if we can manage to live extraordinarily and listen to the Lord's voice, we will stand out from the crowd.

JULY

Be Outstanding

May He strengthen your hearts so that you will be blameless and holy in the presence of our God and Father when our Lord Jesus comes with all His holy ones. 1 Thessalonians 3:13

How do you become a man or woman who stands out? You start seeing yourself as God sees you. How does God see you? Simple: As a Christian, as a Spirit-filled person, washed by the blood and filled with His power.

How do *you* see yourself? Just like everyone else? You know, we are all sinners, and we all make mistakes. But listen again to how God sees you: He says you aren't like everyone else, you don't just fall for sin, and temptation doesn't just besiege you. No, you are different because His Spirit is in you, the blood of Jesus on the cross washed you clean. You are simply different.

Do you realize what happened when you accepted Jesus into your life? You became an extraordinary person. You are different – you are Spirit-filled, you are extraordinary. And God's power is within you.

Become Holy

"You are to be holy to Me because I, the LORD, am holy, and I have set you apart from the nations to be My own." Leviticus 20:26

What prevents you from becoming extraordinary? The biggest obstacle on your path to becoming extraordinary are these words: "I'm going to do what I want, when I want, how I want, with whom I want, because our country doesn't have strong leaders, so I'm my own leader." In other words, I'm going to do what is right in my own eyes. Listen to what Judges 21:25 says: "In those days Israel had no king; everyone did as they saw fit." I can't find a better description for the times we live in.

I often hear people say, "I don't think it's wrong to ..." and then they give a reason for whatever they believe is right. Every time the sentence starts with "I think." It's not about what we think, it's about what God tells us in His Word. He wants us to live holy lives, and the only way to live a holy life is to obey His Word.

Be Wary of Temptations

A person's own folly leads to their ruin, yet their heart rages against the LORD. Proverbs 19:3

How many times have I not seen people wringing their hands, saying, "I don't know how this happened. It was just innocent flirting and text messages, and now it's an affair. I'm going to lose my wife and children!" or "I don't know how it happened, it was just a few innocent drinks after work and now I'm an alcoholic, and I've lost everything."

We must be very careful of seemingly innocent things that we know full well are not so innocent. We mustn't turn a deaf ear to the voice inside us warning us against things with the potential of becoming dangerous. Sin always leads to death, and you'll never overcome sin with excuses. Stay away from the things that you know are wrong, and don't allow your sinful desires to tempt you. Ask the Lord daily to help you.

Anger Destroys

Do not be quickly provoked in your spirit, for anger resides in the lap of fools. Ecclesiastes 7:9

Recently, a motorcyclist was killed when he pushed in front of a motorist in traffic and the person drove over him in a fit of road rage. I also heard about an elderly man who turned in front of another car outside a school; they hooted and shouted and literally wanted to hit the man. Why? They became so angry at others' sins that they completely lost control.

We live in times when people are angry. They're angry because they don't get what they want, they're angry at the country's leaders, they're just mad at everyone and everything.

Ecclesiastes tells us that anger resides in the lap of fools. When you look at the consequences of people's anger, you realize how spot on this Scripture verse in Ecclesiastes is. People destroy their own lives in a moment of rage. If you feel that you're losing control and become easily angered, go to God immediately. Ask Him to take away your anger.

Do the Will of God

We make it our goal to please Him, whether we are at home in the body or away from it. 2 Corinthians 5:9

What are your rules? What is right in your eyes? Who determines right from wrong? I've heard people say, "Don't listen to every word *he* says." Do you know why? Because I think I'm telling the truth as the Bible tells it. And that standard is not always comfortable and popular in today's times. Everything is about what *you* decide and *your* standards. When is enough enough? When you say so. And so it continues …

What is the solution? How are we going to live differently? We must realize that we are to live like Jesus. We must put our own rules and regulations aside and seek His will for our lives. And yes, initially it won't be easy to live according to God's will, but it becomes easier every day. Don't you want to receive the reward of a life lived according to God's will?

Obedience to God

This is love for God: to keep His commands. And His commands are not burdensome, for everyone born of God overcomes the world. This is the victory that has overcome the world, even our faith. 1 John 5:3-4

We don't truly have a clue who we're dealing with and that we're going to stand before God one day.

The following typically happens in relation to fear of the Lord: You commit a certain sin that your parents told you is wrong. You know you shouldn't use that word, but you say it anyway. You wait for a thunderbolt to hit you, but it doesn't happen. Then you use the word again, and again no thunderbolt strikes you down. On the third, fourth and the fifth time you know God is not going to do anything to you. Do you know what has happened here? We've lost our fear for the Lord, because God doesn't come and show His power and wipe us out.

We should obey God's commandments because we love Him, not because we think He's going to punish us. We will one day stand in front of Him and be judged. Don't live in such a way to one day find out our loving God can and does also punish.

Use God's Power

It is God who arms me with strength and keeps my way secure. You armed me with strength for battle; You humbled my adversaries before me. 2 Samuel 22:33, 40

In Gideon's story, he finds an army of 40,000 men. But God says they are too many and reduces the men to 300. Why does He do it? So that everyone would see that He is the One who would make victory possible. Then Gideon overhears one of his soldiers tell the enemy of his dream where he sees God wiping them out.

Do you know the God who resides in your heart? Do you know the Holy Spirit within you? Do you know the meaning of the blood of Jesus over your life? I think most people don't. We are too caught up in our own culture and times that we don't even realize that we have the power of God in us to become men and women of God.

If you believe in the God who also resides in your heart, you automatically become an extraordinary person from the inside. Use His power – it's at your disposal.

Stress and Our Hearts

"Peace I leave with you; My peace I give you. I do not give to you as the world gives. Do not let your hearts be troubled and do not be afraid." John 14:27

Let's touch on the subject of "spiritual cholesterol." What is it exactly? Food, stress, lifestyle and genes are all things that cause physical cholesterol. In the spiritual world, people are equal to food. So you absorb (eat) the things that people do and say, as well as everything that happens around you. Your lifestyle is what you do to yourself.

In the spiritual realm we ask how much you practice spiritually – how healthy your spiritual lifestyle is. Your spiritual genes are of course your image of God.

We must see God in all these situations and ask Him to take control of our lives. There are so many things that happen in life that directly impact us. We must, however, always turn to God for peace. Don't allow the spiritual cholesterol in your heart to steal your joy.

Your Heart Sees Everything

Above all else, guard your heart, for everything you do flows from it. Proverbs 4:23

Your heart is like a sponge that absorbs everything that happens in your life. Your heart, therefore, carries every incident, every answered and unanswered prayer. Everything resides in the heart. I've heard so many stories of young people who were dedicated Christians while in school. They prayed fervently for their parents not to get divorced, but they did. Or they prayed that their mother would triumph over her disease, but she didn't. And so it continues. They pray for the right partner, but get the wrong one.

What is the effect on the heart? Spiritual cholesterol. They become unhappy and struggle in the faith. They find it difficult to deal with all the disappointments of the heart. The question is: What has your heart absorbed so far? Think about it. What has your heart witnessed? Has your heart been disappointed? Hurt? Has your heart become skeptical? Examine your heart.

Guard Your Heart

"But the things that come out of a person's mouth come from the heart, and these defile them." Matthew 15:18

What makes us unclean? Is it outward sins? We can easily point out external sins. Do you remember 20 or 30 years ago that wearing jeans was supposedly sinful? Those trousers were from hell, we were told. There was also a time that women were not allowed to wear makeup. The church hammered on about outward things. According to the church it was a sin. But Jesus says that it's not about outward things, it's what goes on in the heart that's important. From the heart comes adultery, murder, lies, anger, aggression, gossiping – all these things come from the heart. The heart is the source of it all.

It's not the outward appearance like clothing that makes a person unclean. What makes you impure is what goes on in your heart. We spend lots of money on securing our homes and on medical insurance to protect our health. It is not time to invest in guarding your heart?

I Am Born Again

If we confess our sins, He is faithful and just and will forgive us our sins and purify us from all unrighteousness. 1 John 1:9

You may ask: If I'm a born-again Christian, is my heart still full of unrighteousness? I mean, Jesus is in my heart, so where does all the sin come from? Does it still come from my heart? My answer is yes! Jesus perhaps occupies the core of your heart, but He hasn't yet taken over the whole history of your heart.

Remember what I said previously: the heart is like a sponge, it absorbs everything. Yes, Jesus is in your heart and there is now something good in your heart, but guess what? Your whole heart has not been changed. Your heart has been scorched; certain incidents burned your heart. Have you seen a burnt sponge? It becomes as hard as rock and can no longer absorb water. Jesus entered your heart and He is busy taking out the burnt parts. But we must still deal with the hurt, anger and doubt in our hearts. Allow the Lord to cut the scorched parts out so that you can absorb His love.

Do What Is Right before God

Human anger does not produce the righteousness that God desires. James 1:20

Let's talk about the effect of anger in our lives. We read in the verse above that we can't do what is right before God if we're angry. Therefore, we must get rid of the filth and malice that is so prevalent in our lives. Rather, we must humbly accept the Word that God has planted in our hearts.

We think it's because we don't read our Bibles enough, or don't have enough quiet time. We think we don't hear God's voice because we don't go to church often enough. The truth is, you can't hear God's voice when your heart is full of anger. How many people do you know who are only seconds away from exploding? Is it you perhaps? The Scripture verse says that if we are angry, we can't do God's will.

We must take hold of this emotion and deal with the accumulated anger if we want to do His will and have a sensitive heart.

Where Does Anger Begin?

"Now, Lord, take away my life, for it is better for me to die than to live." But the Lord replied, "Is it right for you to be angry?" Jonah 4:3-4

Let's look at the story of Jonah to find out where anger begins. God told Jonah to go to Nineveh and tell the people to repent of their sins and turn back to God. But Jonah didn't want to, because he knew they would ask God's forgiveness and He would forgive them. After Jonah ended up in the fish's belly, he goes to Nineveh and things happen just as he predicted. The people repent of their sins before God and He doesn't destroy the city.

The Scriptures say that Jonah was so angry he wished he were dead. We're all too familiar with such anger. It's pure emotion. That's where Jonah was at, and where we are at. Why do we become so easily angered? Because things don't happen the way we want, because we put our own comfort above everything else, even above 120,000 saved souls.

Mad about Everything

The LORD said to Cain, "Why are you angry? Why is your face downcast? If you do what is right, will you not be accepted?" Genesis 4:6-7

What makes you angry? Everything you can't control. We are angry about the things we want to control, but can't. Can you control politics, the economy, the price of gas? Can you control interest rates, your husband, your wife, your children?

We try really hard, but the truth is we can't control any of these things. You can't even control yourself on some days. And this is the core of anger: We get angry at external things that we see in ourselves, but can't change or control. And because we can't change them, we project our feelings of anger towards everything out there.

Do you know for how long I've tried to control my spouse/children/finances? I can't. And because I can't control it, I'm going to try and control you with my anger. Don't use your anger to feel better about yourself. Work at yourself, lay your shortcomings before God and ask Him to help you control your anger.

What Makes Us Angry?

Jesus entered the temple courts and drove out all who were buying and selling there. He overturned the tables of the money changers and the benches of those selling doves. Matthew 21:12

Let's be honest: We get angry about the wrong things. When last did you become angry because the church didn't function as it's supposed to? When last were you incensed at people not serving God with their whole hearts? When last were you cross with your neighbor for mowing the lawn on a Sunday instead of going to church?

You're angry, but you're angry about the wrong things. You're not angry about your neighbor not having a relationship with the Lord. You're angry because it seems as though he's enjoying life too much. You must get angry for the right reasons. Jesus became angry with those who were buying and selling in the temple. Jesus got mad at the right time, at the right place, for the right reasons. Maybe it's time to follow Jesus' example: Don't get mad about not getting your way. Get mad about God's will no longer being society's first priority.

Accept These Things

The Spirit of the LORD will rest on Him –
the Spirit of wisdom and of understanding,
the Spirit of counsel and of might, the Spirit of
the knowledge and fear of the LORD. Isaiah 11:2

Is there anger inside your heart because of the condition of the country, politics, the economy, your job? Our anger is about many other things, but not about how few people know God. Our anger is not about the things that make God sad: unemployment, poverty, people who have lost their houses in floods. No, our anger is directed at other things. Maybe we must admit to each other that if we want to do God's will, we must practice getting rid of our anger.

The first part of the Serenity Prayer says, "God, grant me the serenity to accept the things I cannot change; courage to change the things I can; and wisdom to know the difference." Isn't that what it's about? This anger? There are things we can't change, and we must accept that. Let us change the things we can.

What Can You Change?

Teach us to number our days, that we may gain a heart of wisdom. Psalm 90:12

You can't say, "My father was like that and my grandfather was like that, so I'm also like that." What needs to change in your life? Something in your relationship with the Lord? Something in your faith? What mustn't or can't change? Ask the Lord for wisdom to see what needs to happen in your life.

Ask the Lord for wisdom to realize which things need changing and start working on these issues. Ask Him to also show you the things that you can't change or control. Ask Him for the peace and serenity to accept this.

Don't waste your energy on situations that you really can't change. Give these situations over to God and free yourself from them.

Who Is Your King?

The LORD is King for ever and ever; the nations will perish from His land. Psalm 10:16

Who is the king of your life? Is God your only King, or do you worship people or material possessions? We read in the Old Testament how God's people wandered away from Him time and again and began worshiping other gods. God had to punish them each time, allowing them to suffer before they repented and turned back to worshiping Him as their King.

Aren't we doing the same thing today? We can't believe that the Israelites fell down before other gods and worshiped them. But don't we also bow before other gods? The idols of today are not statues; they are much more sophisticated. We bow before money or prestige. We see how others make more money than us, and then we also want to be wealthier. We are even prepared to push aside our loved ones if they stand in the way of our ambition. Ask God today if you're not perhaps worshiping other gods.

A God of Forgiveness

You are a forgiving God, gracious and compassionate, slow to anger and abounding in love. Therefore You did not desert them. Nehemiah 9:17

Here's a depiction of mercy and grace to remember: Every time you cry and say you're sorry, each time you say, "Lord, save me," He saves you. What happened every time Israel made a mistake?

What must you do if you realize today that there is another king over your life, another boss or leader, something that rules over you and steals your life? Say you're sorry – even if it's the tenth time – and ask God to forgive you.

The Bible says He will forgive you. Confess your sins and lay them down. Say no to sin with God's help. Don't allow sin to control your life.

Be Obedient

"I gave them this command: Obey Me, and I will be your God and you will be My people. Walk in obedience to all I command you, that it may go well with you." Jeremiah 7:23

Worldly kings are not so merciful as God, because the kings of this world only destroy and take what they can. The problem is that we don't realize the danger we're in until it's too late. We are sometimes under the impression that what we're doing is fine, or the situation we're in is not dangerous.

Most people have walked in a forest at some time or other. Have you ever walked through a forest of thorn trees? You get stuck in the thorns. That's the picture I have in my mind of when another king rules your life. He takes, he tears your clothes apart, he hurts you, he holds you back, he slows you down. It causes pain and discomfort and suffering, and this thorn bush says, "When I'm your king, I'm going to take what's mine." Don't fall for the temptations of the world, rather take heed and keep following Jesus.

Say No to Sin

Blessed is the one who perseveres under trial because, having stood the test, that person will receive the crown of life that the Lord has promised to those who love Him. James 1:12

We all know that money has the potential to ruin lives, but how many of us chase money from dawn till dusk? How often do we prioritize the wrong things in our lives? We all know that wrong relationships can easily get out of hand, but still we continue with our flirtatious text messages. We know it's wrong, but we keep doing it.

Why? Because we get stuck in the thorn bush. We all know the effects of alcohol, drugs, a poor self-image, gossiping. We know these things and we're not naïve enough to think *Yes, but my sins aren't that bad, I know what I'm doing.* The thorn bush warns you that you're going to get hurt: "You're going to get addicted and I'm going to destroy you. You won't ever get rid of me." You know these things, and the Bible also warns us many times. Take heed of these warnings and say no to temptation.

The Idols in Our Lives

Jesus is the true God and eternal life.
Dear children, keep yourselves from idols.
1 John 5:20-21

I get very worried when I see the things that are becoming idols and kings in our lives: work, money, leisure. Idols take and take and take. And if you've allowed the wrong king into your life, it'll be like a thorn bush from which you can't get away. He's not going to tell you, "Tread lightly and sit and rest in my shade."

"No," he says, "Come, so I can take from you."

We have a choice: who will be the king of our lives? What are we chasing after? What do we see? What do we desire? Those things become our kings.

Don't allow these vicious kings a place in your life. Work hard, enjoy what you have – enjoy life – but don't allow money and possessions to become idols in your life.

A Slave to Sin

When you offer yourselves to someone as obedient slaves, you are slaves of the one you obey – whether you are slaves to sin, which leads to death, or to obedience, which leads to righteousness?

Romans 6:16

If sin is your boss you don't have any choice but to obey it. Sin forces you to act if you allow it to control your life. The Greek word for "force" or "compel to do something" is *angareusei*. This is the word used by Jesus in the following verse, "If anyone forces you to go one mile, go with them two miles" (Matthew 5:41).

You sit in front of the computer and you've made up your mind not to watch it anymore, but then *angareusei* whispers in your ear and you're hooked. You say you're not going to drink again, but *angareusei* whispers, "Just one more" and you drink another glass. Choose God as your only Boss and ask Him to save you from addictions in your life. If you're not choosing God, you're choosing *angareusei,* and when *angareusei* is the boss of your life, you're on the path to destruction. Choose to obey God and live.

Put God First

Love the LORD your God with all your heart and with all your soul and with all your strength. Deuteronomy 6:5

Do you know of marriages that just don't work? Two people love each other and they stand in front of the pulpit and say their vows, and what happens not long after? They fight and yell at each other. Why? *Angareusei.* There is someone in charge inside of them, saying, "He doesn't notice you anymore", "Stand up for your rights", "Tell her a thing or two." When you've said these things you immediately regret them. You decide to never fight with your spouse like that again, but what happens two weeks later? *Angareusei* is your boss, your thorn bush. God is not your King.

How do we keep God as the King of our lives? How do we keep Him on the throne of our marriages, so that *angareusei* doesn't become the boss of our lives? We find the answer in Deuteronomy 6. We put God on the throne every day by choosing to put Him first. Put Him in charge of your emotions, and your mind. He must *always* come first.

The King of Your Life

"Love the Lord your God with all your heart and with all your soul and with all your mind and with all your strength." Mark 12:30

Mark 12 is Jesus' answer for you on how to ensure He remains the King of your life when a habit, temper, anger or pride start to play a part. In the rat race of life, when all these things come to the fore, Jesus says, "Love the Lord your God with all your heart and with all your soul and with all your mind and with all your strength."

Who do you put first in your life? Is God your King every day? Let me tell you what happens: We look, we see, we desire, we want something because we think it will make us happy. We chase after it, we find it and it becomes our king.

Two months later we wonder, "How did I get here? I never wanted to be here. I never wanted to be so irritated with my wife and children. What happened?" Can I tell you how? You didn't love God with your whole heart, mind, soul and strength every day.

Forgiveness Is Letting Go

Jesus said, "Do not judge, and you will not be judged. Do not condemn, and you will not be condemned. Forgive, and you will be forgiven." Luke 6:37

One of the main reasons for a lack of spiritual growth is due to guilt over the things you've done, and hurtful experiences you've gone through. You hurt and get hurt as a result of human interaction. This interaction has an effect of the condition of the heart.

Your heart is like a blackboard and everything that happens to you gets written on it. You write down every hurt, pain, every little thing done to you. You must, however, reach a point in your life where you say, "Now I forgive. I'm letting go. I'm done." If you don't do this, your heart will become so hardened that you won't be able to use it. It will be crowded with pain and hurt.

We are going to discuss the issue of forgiveness for the next few days: forgiveness of others and of yourself, and how important this is for your heart and soul.

Sinning against Yourself

When you were dead in your sins, God made you alive with Christ. He forgave us all our sins, having canceled the charge of our legal indebtedness, which stood against us and condemned us; He has taken it away, nailing it to the cross. Colossians 2:13-14

We are well aware of the biblical command to forgive. But what if you're the one trespassing? Even for that you must forgive yourself.

Though we try hard to lead good lives, there are very few people who have never done something they regret. You've treated the love of your life badly, you've neglected your children while they were growing up, you've left important things unsaid and now it's too late. We all have something we blame ourselves for. You struggle with forgiveness even when the people you offended have forgiven you and forgotten the incident.

Jesus died on the cross so that we could be forgiven. How then can we decide that our sins are too big and we don't deserve forgiveness? The acknowledgment of debt has been nullified.

Forgive Others

Bear with each other and forgive one another if any of you has a grievance against someone. Forgive as the Lord forgave you. Colossians 3:13

Just like you've hurt others, they've probably hurt you. Sometimes it's difficult to let go of this hurt. But in various places in the Bible we are commanded to forgive those who have sinned against us.

To forgive others is like carrying a backpack on your back. Every time you forgive it's like taking out a stone – the burden becomes lighter.

It is also important to remember that the type of sin should not influence our forgiveness, whether it was deliberate betrayal by a colleague, or someone who did something to you they were not even aware of. We must forgive for the sake of our own salvation.

Do what Colossians says: Forgive others so that you can be forgiven, but also so that you can free yourself from unforgiveness.

We All Hurt Each Other

You, my brothers and sisters, were called to be free. But do not use your freedom to indulge the flesh; rather, serve one another humbly in love. For the entire law is fulfilled in keeping this one command: "Love your neighbor as yourself." If you bite and devour each other, watch out or you will be destroyed by each other. Galatians 5:13-15

What I like about this passage are the words "one another." We are quick to say, "That guy is snapping at me" or "That person tore me apart with their words." But have you noticed that people who hurt, also hurt others? It's so easy to let your anger take free reign, to let your emotions take over and to say what you want. In the process, though, we tear one another apart. Remember these words: all the hurt, bitterness and pain you've experienced, you've probably also caused someone else. No one is perfect, no one has a perfect personality or nature that never bites back or tears apart.

Therefore, we must look at the message of "Do to others what you would have them do to you" from both sides.

Forgive like Christ

Be kind and compassionate to one another, forgiving each other, just as in Christ God forgave you. Ephesians 4:32

Let's ask the following question: If we've been hurt and we have hurt others, how should we handle it? What should we do? We must forgive, because it's a biblical command.

I spoke to a man recently who sold his holiday home to his friend, but years later he hadn't seen one single cent. His friend moved into the house, and today they're involved in a court case because he can't throw them out. This friend has in fact hijacked his home. The man told me, "You know what I must pray every day? That he doesn't steal my joy and freedom in the Lord. I have to pray this every day, because every day I want to take revenge." His heart is filled with thoughts of anger and revenge, therefore he prays every day that God will help him forgive.

If you battle with anger or thoughts of bitterness and revenge, let this be a lesson to you – pray every day for forgiveness and ask God to help you.

Don't Wait for an Apology

Do not take revenge, my dear friends, but leave room for God's wrath, for it is written: "It is Mine to avenge; I will repay," says the Lord. Romans 12:19

I don't know what other people have done to you, but I know you are probably left with a lot of anger, saying, "But my house was taken" or "My spouse was murdered" or "My child was molested." I'm not talking lightly about these things, but the Bible tells us to forgive. The principle of forgiveness is the same, since God has forgiven us in Christ. But many people say you can only forgive when the other person wants to reconcile. When the hijacker comes to apologize, or the murderer or the guy who stole your money or whoever, only when they say they're sorry will you forgive.

But that's not how forgiveness works. We need to give every hurt over to God, who will judge accordingly. We don't need to wait for the other person to apologize first. Give everything to God, because He will avenge and He will repay. He knows all the secrets of the heart and He will do what needs to be done.

AUGUST

Be Honest about Your Sins

Confess your sins to each other and pray for each other so that you may be healed. The prayer of a righteous person is powerful and effective. James 5:16

Let's talk about the pain and hurt we may have caused. What do we do with the pain we've caused others? We've established the fact that we will often hurt people in the same way we've been hurt. Read today's Scripture verse again and consider the following: The prayers of a person who is in right standing with God are powerful and effective.

We think someone whose relationship with God is good and healthy is an individual who says, "Lord, I've sinned against You, please forgive me. Now my affairs are in order with You." But the Scripture verse says that we must first confess our sins so that we may be healed. It says that we are to confess our sins to each other. So when we confess our sins to a brother or sister in Christ, our relationship with God is automatically restored. The problem here is that we easily confess to God, but not so easily to one another.

Confess your Sins

The Lord our God is merciful and forgiving, even though we have rebelled against Him. Daniel 9:9

Do you know why we confess our sins to God over and over again, but then repeat the sin? Because we haven't confessed to people. Let me give you an example: I get to work, I'm irritated and abrupt, impatient and just nasty. At the end of the day I go home and think about how nasty I was for no good reason.

I drive home and pray and tell God I'm sorry for my bad behavior, and I ask Him to help me to be more patient. I thank Him and ask Him to please forgive me.

But the next day when I get to work I'm irritated and rude. Then I drive home and again ask the Lord's forgiveness; I thank Him and ask Him to take my sins away. And so the process repeats itself day after day. Why? Because we think it's easier to obtain forgiveness from God – at least we don't have to look Him in the eye.

Confess to Each Other

Whoever conceals their sins does not prosper, but the one who confesses and renounces them finds mercy. Proverbs 28:13

Think about yesterday's devotion. What the Bible is saying is that I must go to work tomorrow, call my colleagues together and apologize to them. I've read that when you stand in front of a group two or three times and apologize to a person in front of the group, there's an 80% chance that you won't treat the person badly again. It comes down to the fact that you're going to feel pretty stupid for apologizing for the same thing.

We think it's different to apologize to God. He's merciful, He is God and there's no one to look in the eye. But to stand in front of a man or woman, your children or a colleague yet again and say you're sorry? That brings an end to the sin.

The power of true repentance is not just remorse of the heart before God, but also before those you've treated badly.

Give Your Heart to God

"I will sprinkle clean water on you, and you will be clean; I will cleanse you from all your impurities and from all your idols. I will give you a new heart and put a new spirit in you." Ezekiel 36:25-26

When we've hurt others, we must make things right. I don't know about you, but this is a difficult task. For most people it is difficult to ask for forgiveness.

We make excuses for ourselves: We think that if only people knew our true circumstances, if only they knew where we come from, how our children treat us, they would understand why we act this way. But let's be honest: To give forgiveness and receive forgiveness is not that simple. It's not that easy to stand in front of others and say sorry, or to give the murderer or hijacker to God. It's simply not very easy to just hand it over to Him.

But here's the good news: We serve a God who can change hearts. It might not be easy for us, but with God all things are possible.

God Can Change Your Heart

When you were dead in your sins and in the uncircumcision of your flesh, God made you alive with Christ. He forgave us all our sins. Colossians 2:13

Here's the good news: You don't have to change your heart by yourself. You can't fix the injured parts of your heart.

Some psychologists claim that our issues can start as early as in the womb. So we must go as far back as that to find out what our mother might have said that hurt us. According to the Bible, however, we have a God who, through the work of Jesus Christ on the cross, can go back even farther – to the second and third generation – and can heal.

That's our God. Jesus died on the cross for every hurt, burden and weakness; for every arrow that struck you; for every sword and word that pierced your heart; and for every condemnation and form of human hatred. He did it so that we could have clean hearts and be free from everything that has been done to us, but also from the things we've done to others.

God Sets Us Free

"My friends, I want you to know that through Jesus the forgiveness of sins is proclaimed to you. Through Him everyone who believes is set free from every sin." Acts 13:38-39

In the Bible we find the promise of a new covenant with God that takes all our sins away. He removes the idols, the temptations, and He gives us a new heart. He puts His heart into us and changes our genes. He places His Spirit into us.

What is the result of what Christ has done for you on the cross? You are a slave no more. You don't have to walk around with guilt and pain. You don't have to say, "I've been robbed so many times, and I have so much fear, stress and hurt." Bow down before the cross and say, "I'm leaving everything here." Jesus will take the hurt away and give His heart of love to you. He will pour out His Spirit on you. We must think about what Christ did for us on the cross. The cross is a new covenant filled with inspiration, love, forgiveness, grace and mercy. We live with a heart connected to heaven.

Free from the Burden of Sin

When we were overwhelmed by sins, O LORD,
You forgave our transgressions. Psalm 65:3

What do you have to deal with today? Do you experience guilt because you've hurt people, but haven't made things right? Or do you hold onto unforgiveness because of others who have hurt you?

We must learn to give our guilt to people and our hurts to God. At the moment we are giving God our guilt and our hurt to people. Let me explain: My hurts are what others have done to me. What do I do with it? I project it back onto them. People who are hurt, hurt others. Hurting people take revenge, whereas guilty people give their feelings of guilt to the Lord. God's mercy and grace are endless, so when I'm guilty I want to stand in front of God. When I come to you, I ask that you don't punish me – give me over to God. But when people hurt me, I don't want to give them to God, because He is merciful. He will forgive them, while I would prefer Him to punish them. Don't we all feel like that sometimes?

Our Servitude to God

"Whoever serves Me must follow Me; and where I am, My servant also will be. My Father will honor the one who serves Me." John 12:26

Many of us dream about doing great things for God. We want to do big things for His kingdom, His people, for the souls of the needy. We want to do something for the Lord.

Before we can do big things for God, we must spend time with Him and ask Him what He wants us to do and how. What is the foundation? The direction to follow? Is it biblical and correct to want to do great things for God? To have such a need can sometimes appear humanistic and egocentric, almost as if you see yourself as special, better than others.

You must therefore first examine your motives: Do you want to do great things to make a difference in other people's lives and build God's kingdom on earth, or do you want to do it because you think you're important?

Do Great Things for God

What we preach is not ourselves, but Jesus Christ as Lord, and ourselves as your servants for Jesus' sake. 2 Corinthians 4:5

Have you thought about yesterday's question? Do you want to do great things for God for His honor or for your own?

You say that you want to do something big for the Lord, to see a change. You want Him to use you for what He has in mind for you. I also want it; therefore I turn to the Bible. Can I pray and tell God I want to do great things for Him? I discovered various Scripture verses and the answer was clear. God *does* want us to do great things for His kingdom. When we live a life of service, we show our gratitude towards God for everything He's given us and continues to do for us. There is no better way to say thank You for the life we've received than by bringing others to faith in Him!

It is not wrong to pray and tell the Lord that you would like to do big things for Him. Just make sure your motives are pure.

Make a Difference

"This is to My Father's glory, that you bear much fruit, showing yourselves to be My disciples." John 15:8

Let's look at a few of the Scripture verses that I have come across. One of them is today's Scripture verse, John 15:8. Jesus tells His disciples that He is the Vine and that His disciples are the branches (see John 15:5). God expects us to bear much fruit.

It simply says: Our heavenly Father wants us to do many good things. When we bear fruit, that's exactly what the Father expects.

He doesn't want us to do good things every now and then. He wants us to bear much fruit and make a big difference with the life He has given us. And He wants others to see it and impact their lives.

Use Your Gifts

"He replied, 'I tell you that to everyone who has, more will be given, but as for the one who has nothing, even what they have will be taken away.'" Luke 19:26

We all know the parable of the man who traveled to a distant country and left each of his servants a certain amount of silver. When he returned from his journey, he asked each one what they had done with their money.

The Lord gives each of us spiritual gifts according to our capabilities. And when He returns, He is going to ask what we've done with them. We all know the rest of the story: The servants with the five and two pounds of silver doubled it, and they were well rewarded. The servant who was given one pound of silver buried it and therefore did nothing with it. It was taken away from him and given to the servant with the ten pounds.

With this Scripture verse God is saying that we should make an effort for His kingdom, and dream big dreams.

Serve with Dedication

The fear of the LORD is a fountain of life, turning a person from the snares of death. Proverbs 14:27

Have you cruised through life up till now? If you go to church every now and then, keep your conscience clear for the moment and pray a bit, then yesterday's devotion is for you. You're at risk that the little you devote to God might also be taken from you.

You must decide today for the rest of your life. Tell the Lord, "Lord, use me for something greater. What You've done with and for me, the platform You've given me, Your influence – I want to use it for Your honor." If you don't, it may well be taken from you. We're going to stand in front of the judgment seat and we're going to receive according to what we've given. If you don't use what God has given you, your reward is going to be small. Work hard in God's kingdom so that your gifts won't be taken away.

Through His Power

Now to Him who is able to do immeasurably more than all we ask or imagine, according to His power that is at work within us, to Him be glory in the church and in Christ Jesus throughout all generations, for ever and ever! Ephesians 3:20-21

Ephesians 3:20-21 is one of the Scripture passages where we read that God Himself dreams big dreams and that He can do more than we can think or imagine.

If you think your dreams are big, think about this: God can do immeasurably more than we can think, pray or dream. Let me tell you, God wants to do something great with your life. Do you realize that? God has a plan for your life. He wants to use you for His kingdom. You're not here without reason. Things don't happen by chance.

Your prayers and desires are not coincidental – they are God at work in you. He wants you to take action so that He can show you things even greater than you can imagine.

Glorify His Name

To Him be glory. Ephesians 3:21

Whatever we do, we should do it to bring honor and glory to God. You can't dream big dreams that only benefit yourself. That's selfish.

When I dream big in order to increase my assets and build my own kingdom, it's blatant sin. But if I say to God today, "Lord, I have a dream and a need to do great things for You so that Your name will be glorified, so that people can know You, so that souls may be saved, so that the hungry may be fed, so that broken people can be helped, so that people who have lost hope can find it again. Lord, here I am, use me," then God will use you.

This is the type of dream that He wants us to dream. Whatever you want to achieve with your dreams must always be to honor and glorify the name of God.

Jesus' Ministry Grows

Jesus said, "You believe because I told you I saw you under the fig tree. You will see greater things than that." John 1:50

When you look at Jesus' ministry, you'll see that it grew progressively. He started performing certain miracles, and the miracles became bigger and greater. One of His miracles was so small that the Bible doesn't even describe it as a miracle. This is where Jesus told Nathanael, "You believe because I told you I saw you under the fig tree. You will see greater things than that."

I want to tell you today, if you surrender your life to God, if you give your year planner over to Him and include Him in the setting of your goals, He will use your life and you'll see great things, things you never thought possible.

That's how God operates. He works progressively, all the time. If you can reach one person with whatever you're doing for God, He will help you progress and reach ten people the next time.

Do More

When the wine was gone, Jesus' mother said to Him, "They have no more wine." John 2:3

Jesus and His disciples were at a wedding in Cana when Jesus' mother told Him that the wine was finished. We know the rest of the story and how Jesus turned water into wine.

How does the story end? The master of ceremonies went to the bridegroom and told him, "Everyone brings out the choice wine first and then the cheaper wine after the guests have had too much to drink; but you have saved the best till now" (John 2:10).

That is how Jesus works: He does things bigger and better. He could've made the same wine, but that's not the character of the God we serve. He does great things. When Jesus gave food to the people, there were twelve baskets left over. You should do the same. Don't just stick to the norm – do more every time.

Striving for More

"Very truly I tell you, whoever believes in Me will do the works I have been doing, and they will do even greater things than these." John 14:12

I don't know about you, but I want to put my life in His hands and say, "Here's my life – use it for something greater. Do Your will, Lord."

I don't want to experience the same things over and over, I want to see the Lord do greater things through me. That's who God is, that's what He wants to do with your life. If you've just become a born-again Christian, or have just started having quiet time with God, He's going to do something great for you. You're going to overcome more sins, have more effective quiet time, influence more lives or study the Bible better, because God is progressively letting things grow.

Jesus says that He's going to do even greater things. Jesus doesn't lie; He's never made a promise without keeping it. He's not quick to talk and only think about what He's said afterward. When He says He's going to do even greater things, that's what He means.

Reach Your Full Potential

The fruit of the righteous is a tree of life, and the one who is wise saves lives. Proverbs 11:30

We have the potential to touch our town, our families, our workplace and thousands of lives. Jesus told us to do just that, because we have the potential. Let me ask you a question: What is your dream for the future? What do you still want to achieve?

I'm sure we've all done financial planning. Or you've done academic planning for the future. You want to pass, therefore you will work a bit harder and go to class more often. I'm sure we all desire a better future. Surrender your life into God's hands and say, "Let Your will be done." He wants to do more than you can imagine. He doesn't just want you to pass, He wants you to pass with flying colors *and* influence the other students. He doesn't just want your assets to grow, He wants to give you so much that you can also bless others. He wants a better future for you, He wants it to be the best future ever. That's the God we serve.

Most Important of All

Sitting down, Jesus called the Twelve and said, "Anyone who wants to be first must be the very last, and the servant of all." Mark 9:35

While we're talking about our dreams and plans, we must be careful not to sound arrogant or better than others, as if our plans and dreams are more important than others'.

One day Jesus and His disciples were talking and the disciples started fighting over who was the most important. You can imagine Peter saying, "You know, I've walked on water." Perhaps all of them mentioned something that they'd done and which made them important. Jesus heard the discussion and told them that anyone who wanted to be first must be the last and a servant of all.

Jesus didn't condemn the disciples' question. Rather, He taught them a new definition of what was really important. We must also adapt our thoughts and perceptions according to what is important to God.

Be Willing to Serve

Jesus said, "The greatest among you should be like the youngest, and the one who rules like the one who serves." Luke 22:26

Remember to make sure that your dreams are in honor and glory of God. A person's dream, an earthly dream, is linked to authority and power and self. Jesus put everything into perspective of what is important in His name, and that's to be a servant – someone who doesn't cling to their reputation or pride. Such a person is the greatest servant, said Jesus.

You must therefore change your way of thinking about what it means to do something great for God. You must become a servant. Your dream of doing something big should be about pouring out your life, not how you can enrich your life. You can do more for God by giving your life away. The greatest example is of course Jesus Christ, who gave up His life to save us. Go out today and perform an act of humility for someone else – in this way you will experience the greatest blessing ever.

We All Have Gifts

Each of you has your own gift from God; one has this gift, another has that. 1 Corinthians 7:7

We've all received certain gifts from God. It is, however, your own responsibility to use and develop these gifts to the best of your abilities for the spreading of Gods' kingdom.

I've read the biographies of men and women who've done great things for God in their lifetime. I've examined their characteristics, their principles and their lifestyles. Consequently, I've identified ten points that all of them had in common. Let's look at the first five:

1. They were ordinary people; they weren't born with supernatural gifts and capabilities.
2. They were simple people who loved God.
3. They had a strong character and habits, and were disciplined.
4. They were in control of their thoughts and way of thinking.
5. They read books and mingled with the right people in order to keep their thoughts righteous.

Living for Christ

In Him you have been enriched in every way – with all kinds of speech and with all knowledge. 1 Corinthians 1:5

Yesterday we looked at the first five characteristics of people who stood out in their service to God. Here are the second five:

6. They had the ability to play with words and had an extensive vocabulary.
7. They weren't scared of making sacrifices.
8. They had great faith.
9. They won through people. People were their greatest asset.
10. Their ministry was an adventure, a journey. It was never a punishment or something that was forced on them.

Let me ask you: What is it that keeps you busy from day to day? Think about it. Let's change the question slightly: For which things do you offer up your life?

What Do You Live For?

We are only God's servants through whom you believed the Good News. Each of us did the work the Lord gave us. 1 Corinthians 3:5

What keeps you busy and what things do you dedicate your life to? Every morning starts with a certain amount of energy, because you've had a good night's rest. What things do you spend your energy on? In which things are you investing? What keeps you awake at night, and what do you pray for? What is the first prayer that comes to mind when you think about praying?

Perhaps you've asked the same question in the past week: "What am I doing with my life? Am I busy with God's will for my life, or am I just busy?"

Life passes quickly in a haze of routine, work, money, meetings, another day, another week. And before you know it, another year has passed. The big question is: What are you doing with your time?

Your Future

What I mean, brothers and sisters,
is that the time is short. 1 Corinthians 7:29

Paul knew 2,000 years ago that the time was almost up for doing good deeds. There is far less time than we realize.

Has someone in your circle of friends come to know Christ? For how long are we going to procrastinate and keep ourselves busy with earthly treasures with no eternal value? For how long are we going to make excuses and say "Just one more deal", "Just this one contract", "Just one more deadline", "Just one more relationship"?

When last did you sit quietly with a friend, even for a moment? Have you talked to someone about God recently? About eternal life? Death? About God's purpose and calling? Where are we heading?

We need to become still on a regular basis, and then go and live with purpose. Before you know it, life has passed you by and you haven't done any of these things. Time flies, so don't wait.

Do Something Today

You do not even know what will happen tomorrow. What is your life? You are a mist that appears for a little while and then vanishes. James 4:14

We usually have good intentions: We'll talk about our faith with that person, we'll support this good cause, we'll tell someone about how God cares for us.

Isn't this something you also do? Delaying certain things? The reasons for the delays differ from person to person and some of us are too shy to talk openly about our faith. Others perhaps think that they're not heroes of the faith, so they can't inspire anyone. Or we may be too busy with "life" to get involved.

Whatever the reason or excuse, stop procrastinating. We don't know the future, and tomorrow might be too late. Then we've lost our chance to spread the Good News forever, and to make someone's burden lighter. The time is now to start doing great things for God. Just do it.

Do What You Know Is Right

If anyone, then, knows the good they ought to do and doesn't do it, it is sin for them. James 4:17

I've asked myself about what sinful things I kept myself busy with in the past few weeks. How many times was I aware of the right thing, but I just didn't do it? How many times should I have stood still and listened, given a bit more of my time, a bit more attention, a bit more love, a bit more of myself? But I was too hurried, too busy, had too much to do. We always have good intentions; I will do it tomorrow, next week, next month, next year …

Listen carefully to what James says: If we know the good we ought to do but don't do it, it is a sin. Your failure to talk to someone about God can mean eternal damnation for them. A little bit of attention might just be what someone needs to face the world again.

Don't delay; do what you know is good and right. Don't sin by failing to do something.

The Unknown Future

Why, you do not even know what will happen tomorrow. James 4:14

We have many plans: Today we're going to do this, tomorrow that. But we read in James: You don't even know what will happen tomorrow!

Maybe you're in a wheelchair, maybe something happened to you and you can't talk anymore, or you need someone to help you get dressed and take care of you. You just don't know what the future holds. I don't want to go into detail about sentiment, but ask yourself this question: How long are you going to wait before you start making a difference? Now you might ask: "What are these great deeds?" We think great deeds come with impressive titles, and that someday we'll do something big when we have the authority and power, when money is no object.

We must stop making excuses. You can do something big now. All you need is a heart filled with love.

Become a Servant

"Instead, whoever wants to become great among you must be your servant." Matthew 20:26

We think about greatness and power, but Jesus says in Matthew that whoever wants to become great must be a servant. If you want to lead, you must serve. Jesus says you don't need a platform for doing great deeds. All you need is to be a servant. Serve someone. Do something out of love for another person.

I've wondered about this: Great deeds, a great platform, preaching to thousands of people, doing great things for the Lord and changing lives is wonderful, but do you know what is great in God's eyes? An act of love for someone else who can't necessarily repay you, an act of love from a servant's heart. It is doing something voluntarily and for free simply because you want to serve people.

My question is: How can we perform these acts of service for each other? Think about yourself and find ways of doing something like this for someone else.

Help Each Other

Serve one another humbly in love. Galatians 5:13

What can you do today, without great knowledge or a platform? What can you do to show the Lord that you're serious about giving your life to great acts of love?

It could be things you've never thought about. You can help a complete stranger, by helping them get their groceries into the car while they deal with the screaming baby on their hip. Make someone's burden lighter. If you know of needy people or a welfare organization, see where you can help. Something that looks insignificant to you might change another person's life. It might just change the way that person sees Christians, and you could win a soul for the Kingdom in this way.

You don't have to tell everyone. Just help because God's love urges you to – and you can't help it. Do something for someone who doesn't owe you and who can't repay you.

Wisdom Can Help Others

The LORD gives wisdom; from His mouth come knowledge and understanding. Proverbs 2:6

I've thought about something precious in my life, and that is to share life lessons with other people. I don't know about you, but I've paid dearly for my life lessons. Pain was involved and I've hit my head hard. These were valuable lessons that I learned, and I keep them in my heart.

You don't have to be the person giving advice from dusk till dawn. Let God guide you to say the right things in the right situation. Make time to really talk to people, to tell them of your experiences and what you've learned. It's up to them as to whether to accept or reject your words. The right answer at the right time can mean the difference between life and death for a person.

Be on the lookout for opportunities to share life lessons with others. It might be a small act, but the reward is eternal – for you and for the person you're talking to.

The Poor among Us

"Your prayers and gifts to the poor have come up as a memorial offering before God," the angel said. Acts 10:4

We read in the Bible that those who do kind acts to others who can't return the favor, are blessed.

A kind deed could be to buy food for the needy and give it to them. They could be complete strangers, a poor family in your church, or even a needy colleague. Be tactful – do it in such a way that no one is embarrassed. Be sensitive to people's feelings and don't expect a standing ovation after a good deed.

It needn't just be food – you could offer someone a job, help a student study or assist someone with money for gas. Open your eyes and see the needy people and animals around you, and ask yourself what Jesus would do.

SEPTEMBER

All about Love

If I speak in the tongues of men or of angels, but do not have love, I am only a resounding gong or a clanging cymbal. 1 Corinthians 13:1

The great deed that the Lord wants to see in my life is love. Everything I do must be motivated and driven by love.

If I go for coffee with someone it should be done out of love. If someone steps into my office, I need to treat them with love. When I greet someone on the street, it must be out of love. We are not always that good with love. That's why 1 Corinthians 13 is so important – because when I don't have love, I basically have nothing. I can do marvelous acts of goodwill, but if I don't do them in love, they are meaningless.

Love is patient and kind. It puts other people before ourselves, and forgets about the evil done to us. Love wants only what is best for others, and is joyful when good things happen to them. Love is always patient and keeps believing in good.

Is this your life? Are you motivated by love?

A Life Filled with Love

Dear friends, since God so loved us, we also ought to love one another. 1 John 4:11

I can't emphasize enough the importance of love. Evaluate your life, your love and how much you give of yourself. Do you show neighborly love, even towards people who have offended you?

Everything you do comes back to your heart. What drives you? What keeps you awake? What is your most important prayer at night? Could it be, "Lord, let me love others more, help me to grow in love, let me be sensitive to the needs of people, strangers, those who can't repay any goodness done to them." We are still too concerned about people's identity and what they can do for us. The things we do for them aren't motivated purely from love. Our love for others shows our gratitude towards God. We love because He first loved us.

Don't focus on what others can do for you. Treat others with love and show love towards people in the same way God shows His love for you. Our ability to give, serve and love is the most important thing in this life.

Love for Others

Now these three remain: faith,
hope and love. But the greatest
of these is love. 1 Corinthians 13:13

Our Scripture verse for today tells us that faith is very important on this earth, hope is very important on earth, but love is vitally important.

Listen carefully: What is the only one of these three that you take with you to heaven? You won't need faith in heaven, because you'll see God. You won't need hope, because all promises would be fulfilled. The only thing you take with you to heaven is love.

I think when we get to heaven, we'll be evaluated on one thing, and that's how we loved others on earth.

In heaven we're going to love others and grow in love; therefore, love is the most important. If you want to do great things for God, start with an act of love, because that's the most important thing. Work towards loving others more and more.

In Search of Wisdom

The fear of the LORD is the beginning of wisdom, and knowledge of the Holy One is understanding. Proverbs 9:10

How do we find wisdom in our everyday lives? We all desire God's wisdom. Without His wisdom and guidance we're going to make mistakes. We're going to get hurt and we're going to hurt others. We certainly need God's wisdom.

Wisdom starts by serving the Lord. The first and most important principle of wisdom is to work at your relationship with the Lord. Every time you read your Bible, pray or go to church, you are investing in your relationship with Him.

We speak of "in search of wisdom" as if it's an object that we can obtain. Wisdom is a Person, and God is wisdom. Jesus is the wisdom of God and therefore we mustn't search for a parcel or a book or something that will fall from the sky. What are you searching for? It should be a Person, a relationship with the Wise One. If you serve God, you become wiser, because the Wise One will influence your life.

Be Wise in Everything

Blessed are those who find wisdom, those who gain understanding. Her ways are pleasant ways, and all her paths are peace. She is a tree of life to those who take hold of her; those who hold her fast will be blessed. Proverbs 3:13, 17-18

If you are searching for God's wisdom, it's important to remember that this wisdom should touch all areas of your life. We must therefore not divide our lives into compartments, and think wisdom has only to do with our relationship with the Lord.

We must use godly wisdom when it comes to our finances, and allow Him to guide us to make wise decisions. We cannot exclude God in our relationships – we need wisdom to act in the right way and treat others correctly. We need God's wisdom in bringing up our children. We need wisdom at work – we must ask God every day to give us wisdom to be honest and righteous, to treat others as we want them to treat us.

Ask God for His wisdom in every area of your life, and experience His blessing and guidance.

Rest in the Lord

Return to your rest, my soul, for the LORD has been good to you. Psalm 116:7

To just do nothing for a while has almost become a sin in today's world. To rest is seen as a weakness, a lack of ambition. But the Lord tells us to rest. Think about Psalm 23: "He makes me lie down in green pastures, He leads me beside quiet waters, He refreshes my soul. He guides me along the right paths for His name's sake" (Psalm 23:2-3). What a wonderful thought that the Lord Himself strengthens and refreshes us.

In order for that to happen we must become quiet before Him. Put away your phone, your iPad, your laptop. There's nothing more important in life than becoming quiet before the Lord and listening to His voice. We must relax, and we must rest. It's not healthy to be busy all the time. The world won't come to a standstill if you relax for a few minutes. It might have the desired effect: you will become more focused, see new solutions to problems, become more patient with loved ones. Be still – you can only win.

The Right Crowd

Stay away from a fool, for you will not find knowledge on their lips. Proverbs 14:7

The people with whom you spend your time will determine to a large extent who you become and how you behave. Therefore it is important to choose your friends wisely.

Do your friends exert a constructive influence on your life, or must you constantly take care not to get dragged down by them? Ask yourself then if such a friendship is worth it.

There are also relationships in our lives over which we have no control – people who must be in your life out of sheer necessity. If you find that these aren't healthy relationships, ask the Lord for wisdom. Don't get dragged down by their actions. Don't allow others to influence your behavior – let the Lord determine how you will act, and stay on the right path.

It's not an easy task, but relationships must be a blessing in our lives, not a curse. Evaluate your relationships today!

Choice Silver

The tongue of the righteous is choice silver, but the heart of the wicked is of little value. Proverbs 10:20

Actions with words have an immense influence on people. You can wound someone for the rest of their lives, or you can encourage and build them up with your words.

You must watch what you say. We say things before we think, and then we regret it. It takes a lot of self-control not to give your tongue free rein. We often want to correct someone, put them in their place or get our viewpoint across. We'll only be able to make our words count with God's help.

Rather, let people wonder why you are keeping quiet, instead of saying the wrong things that can never be unsaid.

Ask the Lord to help you today to make your words choice silver, and ask Him to guide you in everything you say.

Don't Sin with Your Words

Sin is not ended by multiplying words, but the prudent hold their tongues. Proverbs 10:19

If you talk a lot, chances are good you're going to sin. If you are cautious with your words, chances are good that you're going to sin less.

We all have a need to talk. Sometimes we say anything that comes to mind. I think the principle here is simple: talk less. People often expect you to say something, but if you have nothing positive and constructive to add, keep quiet. Don't say the wrong thing and sin just because you were under pressure to speak.

I'm also searching for wisdom in my life. It's not always easy, because people will tell you things and expect a wise answer. Nonetheless, Proverbs teaches us to rather keep quiet. Talk less, and don't say everything that comes to mind. If you can control your tongue, you are wise.

Words like Daggers

The words of the reckless pierce like swords, but the tongue of the wise brings healing. Proverbs 12:18

I think we've all experienced this. Someone said something to you that has hurt deeply. And sometimes we carry the hurt with us for years. How many times has someone said something to you and it pierced like a sword? But more importantly: How many times have *you* said things that hurt? How many times have you said things and wished you could take them back? Maybe you've even hurt someone without realizing it.

Proverbs says that if you can control your tongue, it will bring healing. How I pray this, how I pray that my words would be words of healing, not only from the pulpit, but in my friendships, my marriage, my relationships, with my children.

We must speak words of healing towards all people. The author of Proverbs says the tongue of the wise brings healing, if we can just control our tongues.

The Right Words

From the fruit of their lips people enjoy good things. Proverbs 13:2

If you work in sales and marketing, you'll know how important it is to use the right words. How do you close a deal; how do you convince someone to buy your product? This is of course by using the right words.

The Scripture verse above doesn't just apply to salespeople, it applies to everyone. Words can have an immense influence on our lives. Just as using the right words in business can help you prosper, so the right words in your relationships can also help you thrive. Think about the greatest scene in any movie – it's where the guy declares his undying love to the girl, is it not? Just as beneficial as words can be, they can also tear apart. Why aren't all people being promoted, and why do some relationships not work out? Because of wrong words that hurt and tear down.

Only speak words that can help you and others prosper. If you're in doubt, keep quiet.

The Words of the Lord

Whoever gives heed to instruction prospers, and blessed is the one who trusts in the Lord. Proverbs 16:20

We've talked about the importance of words. Our words can break down or build up. We can say wise things to someone, or we can say something foolish. We are constantly aware of words, be it our own words or the words of others.

The most important words to listen to, however, are of course the words of the Lord in the Bible. It's important to study the Bible to know exactly what is expected of us in life. The Lord's words are not just a bunch of rules to obey. His words offer wisdom and support. His words give strength and encouragement, and help us to live for Him and honor Him.

We find His wisdom in the Bible, and we can apply this wisdom to our everyday lives. Like we see in Proverbs, whoever gives heed to God's instructions will be blessed.

Rather Safe Than Sorry

Do you see someone who speaks in haste? There is more hope for a fool than for them. Proverbs 29:20

Hurtful words can never be taken back. You can apologize and try to compensate in some way, but what you've said is said. Have you ever wished you could take back your words? We are all guilty; we've all said things that were better left unsaid. We are quick to speak, and we don't think about our words until afterward. Whether you've deliberately hurt someone with your words, or said something in an unguarded moment, you can't take it back.

To say the wrong thing is like cutting open a feather pillow – all the feathers are picked up by the wind and blown around. "Sorry" is then trying to pick them up again. It's just not possible. Spoken words can never be unsaid.

Say the right words so that it won't be necessary to apologize. Say constructive things, and think before you speak.

The Power of Words

The tongue has the power of life and death, and those who love it will eat its fruit. Proverbs 18:21

What do your words sound like? Your conversations? Do you say positive things, or do you tear down with your words? Have you noticed that you do this, or do you need to pay extra attention to what you say?

Each one of us must evaluate our own situation. You must listen to yourself and ask yourself if you can be proud of what you've said. Is it an area in your life that needs work? The tongue and our words have been touched on by many authors of the Bible. They speak mostly about our words and what they should be like. We should listen to what these authors have written about the tongue, because our lives consist of words, which are carried over to the next generation.

You can develop love in a person's heart for the things of the Lord, or you can alienate them completely. Watch what you say, and speak words of life.

Count Your Words

"I tell you that everyone will have to give account on the Day of Judgment for every empty word they have spoken." Matthew 12:36

In this verse, it is Jesus who is speaking. Now if there is one Scripture verse to highlight in the Bible, it's this one. We will have to give account for every empty or frivolous word we've said.

Jesus said that every word spoken in secret will be shouted from the rooftops. What was He referring to? Our words. We must watch what we say, the comments we make about other people.

I've searched for a description of what empty and frivolous words mean exactly. It might be a joke or something silly you've said.

An empty word is a word spoken without thinking or concentrating, and without considering the consequences. It's when you rush your words without thinking. Jesus warned against this, and it's a warning to take heed of.

Avoid Foul Language

Do not let any unwholesome talk come out of your mouths, but only what is helpful for building others up according to their needs, that it may benefit those who listen. Ephesians 4:29

Aren't we all guilty? Who can honestly say that foul language has never escaped their lips?

Sometimes we want to apologize for what we've said, since it just slipped out. "Ouch" is really not strong enough to express our feelings when we hit our finger with a hammer. Nonetheless, there is no excuse for foul talk, especially from a child of God. You can't praise Him one moment and curse someone the next with the same mouth!

Think about what you're saying: Will it be an embarrassment to you if your parents, boss, pastor or children know every word that comes from your mouth? Or are you going to be proud because your words influence others positively?

Think before you speak; don't say things you'll later regret.

Stop Gossiping

Whoever conceals hatred with lying lips
and spreads slander is a fool. Proverbs 10:18

Sometimes a story is just too good to keep to yourself, not so? Or sometimes we just say bad things about someone to give them a taste of their own medicine. The Bible is clear: You're a fool if you gossip.

Gossip is born of a sinful heart and if you gossip you're a messenger of Satan. Gossip also comes from a jealous heart. It's easier to gossip about someone than to be happy for them. Even if the story is true, ask yourself what the motive is behind telling the story. In most cases it's pure sensationalism. You can't gossip under the banner of "helping" someone – if you really want to help the person, go to them and offer your help.

Stop gossiping today, and never again say anything about someone else that you don't want them to say about you.

Be Full of Cheer

A cheerful heart is good medicine, but a crushed spirit dries up the bones. Proverbs 17:22

We often think everything about religion is supposed to be serious and without humor. That's how genuine Christians live, isn't it? And serious things suit serious people. However, this idea about faith is actually wrong. We're allowed to be joyful and merry and cheerful – after all, we have so much to be thankful for! How can we marvel at God's wonderful creation and not be cheerful?

The Lord wants us to be happy – He wants us to rejoice in His love and in Him. He wants us to find joy in our gifts, our loved ones, in each and every day. There is of course a difference between rejoicing and being frivolous. There are certainly specific occasions when we need to be serious, but not always.

Rejoice, and let others see your joy – show them how much joy and love God brings into your life.

A Joyful Life

I know that there is nothing better for people than to be happy and to do good while they live. That each of them may eat and drink, and find satisfaction in all their toil – this is the gift of God.
Ecclesiastes 3:12

God is joy. Jesus was anointed with the oil of joy; therefore joy must be part of your life, and the joy of the Holy Spirit must be within you.

In Galatians 5:22-23 we read that a fruit of the Spirit is joy. As Christians we must live joyful lives.

The psalmist says that, "You will make known to me the path of life; You will fill me with joy in Your presence, with eternal pleasures at Your right hand."

When we know that the Spirit is within us and that God is with us we are filled with joy. Even when times are tough, our joy in the Lord remains.

A Grateful Heart

Nor should there be obscenity, foolish talk or coarse joking, which are out of place, but rather thanksgiving. Ephesians 5:4

We've talked about dirty language and how it isn't suitable for a child of God. What is fitting for God's children? The answer is gratitude to God.

We can only be thankful when we realize what wonderful gifts we've received from the Lord. We must always be focused on giving thanks. We should be thankful for the small things in life: when someone does something nice for you, when you receive a small gift, when you receive a favor. If we can't appreciate and be thankful for the small and insignificant things, we won't be thankful for the big things in our lives.

If you can't say with a clean conscience, "Thank You, Lord, for the lovely visit", "Thank You for my loved ones", "Thank You for this day", then something is very wrong. Then you must examine your heart and see what prevents you from being thankful.

Do you have a thankful heart?

Don't Be a Fool

Fools find no pleasure in understanding but delight in airing their own opinions. Proverbs 18:2

Aren't we all fools concerning this Scripture verse? We all love airing our own opinions.

We mustn't become so obsessed with our own opinions that we distance ourselves from others' advice. Fools like the sound of their own voices very much – there is no place for other people's opinions in their lives. They tell their stories to everyone – whether they're interested or not.

Don't be foolish. Take note of your words and force yourself to keep quiet if you're taking over the whole conversation. Be sincerely interested in others. Share their joys and sorrows; support them and put their needs first.

It is so much better when someone comes looking for you, rather than trying to avoid you because everything is always about you. Ask the Lord to help you talk less, and be aware of when the conversation revolves around you only.

Keep Your Lips Clean

Whoever would love life and see good days must keep their tongue from evil and their lips from deceitful speech. 1 Peter 3:10

The "deceitful speech" that we read about here is nothing other than gossip. It's a subject we read about more than once in the Bible. It is clear that the Lord wants to address this issue. We must keep our lips from gossiping.

Gossip destroys many good things in life. It destroys relationships, friendships, trust. At a stage people may want nothing to do with you. They don't know if they might be the next victim of your tongue.

If you want a long life with many friends, stop gossiping. If you like gossiping, ask the Lord to cleanse your heart. Sometimes it will even be necessary to apologize to the people who you have gossiped about. Let God guide you.

Control Your Tongue

Likewise, the tongue is a small part of the body, but it makes great boasts. Consider what a great forest is set on fire by a small spark. James 3:5

We know that we should control our tongues, but do we? I apply the principle of "listen and learn" to my life.

The "listen" I'm referring to is to listen to yourself. It might sound strange, but learn to listen to yourself. Do you know how much you can learn by doing this? And how much more when you recall a conversation you've had and think, "I said something really silly. I hope I didn't hurt the person."

Listen to yourself. We talk on the phone, we're busy, and we never become quiet. We don't take the time to look and listen to what we're saying to others.

Your children are mirrors of how you act. Look and listen to them when they copy you. How do you drive, talk, reprimand, make jokes? Get to know yourself.

Listen to What Others Say

God gives wisdom, knowledge
and happiness. Ecclesiastes 2:26

We must learn from others by listening to what they say. The Lord places wise people in our lives; we don't have to follow them like slaves, but we should listen to them and learn from them.

I've had the privilege of listening to a wise person. When he finished speaking I said to the others, "Wow, have you noticed how wisely this man chooses his words?" Every word was chosen perfectly, and made so much sense. He had the gift of saying a lot by using only a few words. And the things he achieved in his life have been remarkable.

You can listen and learn from a person like this. Then you can decide for yourself if you want to walk that same road. Other people's words can teach you a lot in life.

Guard Your Mouth

Set a guard over my mouth, LORD; keep watch over the door of my lips. Psalm 141:3

Do you know what happens when you ask the Lord every day to set a guard over your mouth? It makes you sensitive to every word you say.

When you've prayed this prayer, you can be reassured that you've prayed about the matter; you must now start listening and thinking before you speak, because there is a guard over your mouth. It is amazing how much power such a short and simple pray has.

Pray this prayer every day – however, it should not become a repetition of the same words that later mean nothing. This prayer must become your way of thinking. You must focus on the guard over your mouth so that every word you speak brings only glory and honor to the Father. Ask Him to guard your mouth.

Guard Your Heart

"The mouth speaks what the heart is full of." Matthew 12:34

You can control your tongue by controlling your thoughts and what is in your heart.

Our problem sometimes happens because of what goes on in our hearts and thoughts. If you fill your heart and mind with bad language, what do you think will come out of your mouth next time you get a fright? What will come out? Whatever is already in your heart. If you watch violent movies and it's one foul word after the next, what do you think will come out of your mouth when you're mad? Whatever you put in your heart and thoughts.

It's good to ask the Lord to guard your mouth and to control whatever comes out, but it's also equally important to control what goes in. You must fill your heart and thoughts with the living Word of God, with things that are beneficial and constructive and good.

Give Heed to God's Words

The one who gets wisdom loves life;
the one who cherishes understanding
will soon prosper. Proverbs 19:8

This Scripture verse turns everything around. What will come out of my mouth when I listen to God's words, and fill my heart and mind with the Scriptures?

What will come out are all the things that I put in: the wisdom and love of the Lord. The more you fill yourself with His living words, the easier life-giving words will flow from your mouth. The more you fill yourself with death, the more death will come out your mouth.

First change a few of your habits, and then change your vocabulary. It's simple; sometimes you just need to switch off the TV, close the book or end the conversation. Sometimes you must decide that you don't want these things in your life. Pursue the things that lead to love, mercy, forgiveness, truth and wisdom.

The Lord Is with You

"Have I not commanded you? Be strong and courageous. Do not be afraid; do not be discouraged, for the LORD your God will be with you wherever you go." Joshua 1:9

Isn't this just the most wonderful promise? How can anyone be afraid when the Lord Himself says that He will be with you? Don't be afraid.

We're scared of many things. We're scared of the unknown. We're scared of darkness, but also of the light. We're so afraid of things that we become completely paralyzed by fear and can't enjoy life anymore. We're scared of trying new things, and stagnate in an unhappy and boring life. We then become people who look at the world with fear, even though we long to be part of this world. We know we're missing out on a lot of joy, but our fears hold us back.

Maybe you think the Lord hasn't told you what He told Joshua. But that's where you make a mistake. It's in the Bible, and therefore He is also addressing you. Stop being afraid; the Lord is with you.

Conquer Your Fears

The LORD is with me; I will not be afraid. What can mere mortals do to me? The LORD is with me; He is my helper. Psalm 118:6-7

There are many types of fear in the world. There are "good" fears – the type that prevents us from doing silly things, thereby keeping us safe. Then of course, there are bad fears – the type that are completely irrational and steal our joy.

Social phobias do also exist. Some people are so afraid of social interaction that it controls their whole life. Some of these phobias might start with something like being overly timid when greeting others, which might eventually result in such a person avoiding all contact with others. They become isolated from the world and live like a hermit. A phobia like this is a sad thing, because the psalmist rightly asks, "What can mere mortals do to me?" If you know of someone who has developed timidity towards other people, or if you feel that you are on a lonely road yourself, ask the Lord to make you strong. He is with you and He will help you.

More Than a Conqueror

"I have told you these things, so that in Me you may have peace. In this world you will have trouble. But take heart! I have overcome the world." John 16:33

The Lord never promised that we'd go through life without any difficulty. It's a fact that terrible things happen to people. People do unthinkable things to each other.

When something bad happens to a person, it often influences the rest of their life. We build walls around ourselves to protect us from more pain. We battle to trust people and situations. It's totally understandable – we can't judge others if we've never experienced what they've been through. In many cases we think the walls they've erected are justified.

But Jesus tells us that He has overcome the world with its pain and brokenness, and we are more than conquerors through Him. Give your hurt and pain to the Lord and set your trespassers free. Remember, you can only do it with His strength. Take back your life back in His name and know that you're more than a conqueror.

OCTOBER

Trust in the Lord

The LORD will be the sure foundation for your times. Isaiah 33:6

Many of us have been hurt by life; as a result we build high walls around ourselves to protect us from getting hurt again. People don't trust each other anymore. The fear of rejection has almost become a phobia – we're too scared to love, we're too scared to give our honest opinions, we're too scared to be ourselves, all because we're too scared of being rejected and because we don't want people to come too close. We are reticent and wary to give of ourselves. Accordingly, we remain lonely.

Our fear of rejection is sometimes so overwhelming that it influences our relationship with God. We think that if we give too much of ourselves, God will also reject us or push us away. But God is not like us; He will never reject or humiliate us. We read repeatedly in the Bible that we can trust in God; He will never leave us or forsake us. You can give yourself completely over to God and trust Him – He'll never reject you.

Losing Your Religion

Do not throw away your confidence;
it will be richly rewarded. Hebrews 10:35

I know someone who wanted to become a missionary after school – something he excelled at. He wanted to attend university and study theology, but he wasn't selected. He lived close to God, but this event hurt him deeply, so much so that he now wants nothing to do with the church.

It is tragic that a decision he made years ago influenced his whole outlook on life. This happens to many people today. We get hurt and we believe it comes from the Lord. We struggle to distinguish between what people do and what God wants to do for us.

Remember that God only wants what is best for us. We must take care not to renounce our faith because of hurt in our lives. Hold on to God. If you feel your faith is weak, ask God to strengthen you.

Don't Hide from God

Adam answered, "I heard You in the garden, and I was afraid because I was naked; so I hid." Genesis 3:10

What happened when Adam and Eve sinned? They were afraid of God, afraid of interacting with Him. They hid, and thought that He wouldn't find them.

This "hiding away" is something people are doing more often today. It is possible to be in a relationship, and still hide. You can meet people and shake hands, give hugs, smile and be friendly, but still hide.

You can hide from people and only reveal bits of yourself, but you can't hide from God.

The main reason why we hide from God is because of our sin. We have a guilty conscience and instead of confessing our sins, we want to hide. We don't realize that it's much easier to just confess our sins so that we can live in His light once again. Stop hiding from God today.

We All Need Someone

Rejoice with those who rejoice; mourn with those who mourn. Live in harmony with one another. Romans 12:15-16

People need each other. It doesn't matter if you don't trust people, or if you've been hurt or whatever the case may be – everybody needs somebody. No one can go through life alone.

Unfortunately, people become more and more isolated from others. We don't live in close and intimate relationships anymore. Social media as such is not the culprit – in fact, we are able to spread the Good News to the ends of the earth, and knowledge is just the push of a button away. Our loved ones are only a Skype call away.

However, there are people who have become so obsessed with what's happening on their mobile phones and iPads that the beauty of life is passing them by. They are so focused on that little screen that despite lots of real-life friends, they're still alone. We weren't created to be alone – we need human interaction. Look up from your computer screen for once and just live.

In Our Father's Arms

May the Lord make your love increase and overflow for each other and for everyone else, just as ours does for you. 1 Thessalonians 3:12

Research has shown that baby monkeys would rather go without food and milk than without physical touch from their mother. Few things are as important to a child's development as physical touch.

Of course it doesn't just apply to babies. Adults don't always want to admit it, but they need physical touch too. A marriage requires showing affection; friends need hugs from each other; and children need a loving touch from their parents. Sometimes a hug at the right time can mean so much more than words.

In the same way we want to embrace others in times of need, our heavenly Father also wants to hold us close to Him. There is no better place in this world than to be in the Father's arms. Just as you long for people to support you in times of sorrow, you must long for your Father. Allow Him to comfort you and feel safe in His arms.

Someone Who Accepts You

Jesus said, "I do not accept glory from human beings." John 5:41

From childhood we tend to be scared of rejection. Whether it's small children crying because Mom or Dad reprimanded them or because they fought with their friends, or teenagers who feel that they don't fit in, these things are all born from the fear of being rejected. Some people would even give up their own identity just to fit in with the crowd.

Jesus said in the gospel of John that He is not concerned about the glory of human beings. He says that you won't receive glory and honor from God if you're concerned about what people think of you.

You can't receive God's honor if you've shaped your identity to please people. Allow God to shape you and let your biggest priority be to seek honor from Him.

Second Chances

If you bite and devour each other, watch out or you will be destroyed by each other. Galatians 5:15

We can hurt each other deeply. We say things thoughtlessly or we wound others intentionally. We make silly jokes and someone takes it personally. We do something that brings great harm to another person. We hurt deliberately and we hurt accidentally. The point is: we hurt each other.

It's not always easy, but we can't allow our hurt to dominate our lives. At some point we need to rise above our pain and give people a second chance. We must be willing to forgive each other, especially if the person apologizes. Sometimes it is also necessary to forgive them even if they don't apologize.

Unfortunately it is human nature to "bite and devour each other" – and we must watch out that we don't hurt others. Also remember that it's important to forgive when someone trespasses against you.

Think before You Speak

The tongue has the power of life and death, and those who love it will eat its fruit. Proverbs 18:21

It's a terrible thing to say, but people are mean. Few of us have not suffered from the cruelty of others. One almost wants to say, such is life. Just accept it.

But we can't. We can't just accept that we live in a world where people "bite and devour" each other. We can also not sit and wait for things to change. As the saying goes, "Be the change you want to see in the world." Start with the way you treat others, your words. Do you speak words that hurt and wound? Are people scared of your sharp tongue? Or do you speak words of life and love?

Think before you speak. Ask the Lord to help you control your tongue. Rather keep quiet if you have nothing good to say. Be a soft-spoken person, and see how people start to change.

When Forgiveness Is Difficult

Be kind and compassionate to one another, forgiving each other, just as in Christ God forgave you. Ephesians 4:32

We know now that people are cruel and that the world is full of pain. We've all been hurt. It's also true that some people have to endure far worse things than the rest of us. We are then quick to tell them to just forgive and move on.

But it's certainly not that easy. We need to understand people's inability to forgive, though it doesn't mean we should just leave the matter. People who have been hurt often have a long road ahead before they'll find forgiveness in their hearts. We must support them and not force them to forgive.

What we can do is to pray for them. We can ask the Father to heal their wounds and strengthen them to be able to forgive their trespassers. If you know of people who are battling hurt and pain in their lives, dedicate them to God in prayer.

Don't Live in Fear

May Your salvation, God, protect me. Psalm 69:30

Nobody is exempt from pain. Yet although it's a fact that we'll get hurt at some point in life, we can't allow our future fears to control us.

Yes, we live in challenging times, but too many people live in fear. You read a story on Facebook (which is not true in most cases) and you find another reason to be afraid. We can't give our fears that much power.

We mustn't allow others to steal our joy because of stories, which are often false. We must say with the psalmist, "May Your salvation, God, protect me," and believe it. Live as if you believe this. Stop being afraid of invisible dangers and place your life in God's hands.

God Will Heal

May the Lord of peace Himself give you peace at all times and in every way. 2 Thessalonians 3:16

Let's start on our road to recovery and healing. How can we be free from the pain and hurt in our lives? Like we've seen before, it's not an easy road, but it is possible.

We serve a wonderful God. When bad things happen to us, we are often tempted to turn our backs on Him and blame Him. But these painful times are the times when we need our Lord the most. He can heal us and give us peace.

We must unlock our hearts and allow Him inside. It's not something that happens overnight. Don't be impatient if you feel that you've not reached complete healing. Allow God to work in your heart and life in His own time to bring you healing and peace.

The only thing you need to do is open yourself up to the wonderful ways that His love can work in your life.

Freed from the Past

"Forgive, and you will be forgiven." Luke 6:37

For many people who have been hurt, it's unthinkable to forgive their offenders. It is, however, the only way to be freed from the past. Some people think that if they forgive those who trespassed against them, the offenders will "get away" with their wrongful actions. But this is not true. Forgiveness is more about what it means to you.

Some people say that you must say out loud every day that you've forgiven the person who hurt you. You must do this even though it feels like you're far from forgiving that person. At first it is going to be difficult, but after a while – even if it means years – you'll realize that you mean what you say. And then you will experience freedom from your pain.

It is so important to realize that you can't live an abundant life until you forgive.

When You Feel Abandoned

At my first defense, no one came to my support, but everyone deserted me. May it not be held against them. 2 Timothy 4:16

"Everyone deserted me." Isn't this the story of our lives? Sometimes it feels like we're all alone and need to fight for what we want in life. You can, however, easily fall prey to becoming bitter and later start cursing everybody.

Listen to what Paul is saying, "May it not be held against them"! What a wonderful, forgiving heart! We must also have such an attitude.

We often want God to punish people who sin against us. We silently curse them and wish nothing good for them. We've been hurt deeply and want revenge. But not Paul. He forgives them; he doesn't even want to give them over to God to punish them.

That's how great God's love for people is. Let us take this lesson from Paul to heart.

Forgive and Forget

Bear with each other and forgive one another if any of you has a grievance against someone. Forgive as the Lord forgave you. Colossians 3:13

You can't forget, especially not right away. If you've been hurt or offended, you'll remember it for a long time. But listen to this: If you forgive with a sincere heart, you'll be able to forgive. Isn't this a wonderful thought?

If you're purposely trying to forgive someone, you will find a way to do it. And if you're working at not being reminded of your pain all the time, you'll be able to do so through God's strength. It's easy to hold on to hurt, but you deny yourself so much joy. What are you afraid of? Why are you hesitant to forgive?

Take your doubts to the Lord and ask Him to open your heart. Work with Him through your pain and ask Him to set you free from your past. Some things are just not worth holding on to.

The Ten Commandments

And God spoke all these words. Exodus 20:1

For the next few days we'll be discussing the Ten Commandments and the Old Testament. Is it still relevant today? Many people think that what was written in the Old Testament is exactly that – old. It doesn't apply to us anymore. It's just a piece of history, something that became obsolete when Jesus was born.

Many people argue that we can no longer be saved by "the Law," and therefore need not live according to it. Such people argue that we were freed from them when Jesus came to earth – we are thus saved by grace.

The Old Testament, however, is still the Word of God and each word has meaning and stands fast. Thus the Ten Commandments are still relevant. We must live, love and learn according to it.

The Old Testament Is Ratified

"Do not think that I have come to abolish the Law or the Prophets; I have not come to abolish them but to fulfill them." Matthew 5:17

The Old Testament is as inspired by and filled with the things of God as the New Testament. We cannot separate the two. We can also not give more authority to the one than the other.

Listen to what Jesus says in verses 18-19: "For truly I tell you, until heaven and earth disappear, not the smallest letter, not the least stroke of a pen, will by any means disappear from the Law until everything is accomplished. Therefore anyone who sets aside one of the least of these commands and teaches others accordingly will be called least in the kingdom of heaven, but whoever practices and teaches these commands will be called great in the kingdom of heaven."

What does this mean for us? Jesus says that when you are saved by grace, you won't be able to do anything but live according to His will. The Old Testament and the laws are one thing: a revelation of the will of God to people.

Rules and Regulations

Moses summoned all Israel and said:
Hear, Israel, the decrees and laws
I declare in your hearing today. Learn them
and be sure to follow them. Deuteronomy 5:1

There are many rules in the Old Testament that we don't follow anymore. So how are we supposed to know what and what not to do? Many of God's rules in the Old Testament were educational and moral rules. God wanted to educate His people. They were to learn about Him and get to know Him.

Think about a small child who learns to walk. What do they hear most often? "No." "Be careful." "Don't do this." "Don't do that." Is it because you hate your child? No, absolutely not! You love your child and want to protect them; therefore you lay down certain rules to prevent harmful behavior.

It works exactly the same way with God. He loves us and wants what's best for us; therefore He gave us rules. This is not to punish us or take fun out of life, but to keep us safe. We are safe and protected when we obey God's rules for our lives.

How We Ought to Live

At that time I stood between the LORD and you to declare to you the word of the LORD, because you were afraid of the fire and did not go up the mountain. Deuteronomy 5:5

Because the Israelites were in Egypt for such a long time, they became accustomed to the Egyptians' habits and customs. When the Lord saved them from Egypt He knew their faith was still inside them, but they didn't have a relationship with Him. Therefore He had to teach His people right from wrong.

We are also God's people, but, just like the Israelites, we also accept the customs of the world. We have faith in our hearts, but we don't know right from wrong and we don't have a living relationship with God. That's why we still have the Ten Commandments today to guide us. God gave us these rules because He loves us. Read the Ten Commandments carefully: Is any one of them unrealistic or unfair? No. They show us a safe way to live. We must thank the Lord for His love and care, and that by His commands we are kept safe.

No Other Gods

"You shall have no other gods before Me." Exodus 20:3

One must remember that the Israelites didn't live in a monotheistic society, where the teaching or belief was that there was only one God. Most tribes in those times worshiped many gods – in fact, the Old Testament was written in the context of polytheism. Therefore it didn't come naturally to the Israelites to worship only one god.

The command in today's verses taught the Israelites that there was only one God. Personal obedience was required of them to only allow this one God into their lives and worship Him alone.

This command is still applicable today. God demands obedience from each of us. He cannot be one of the many gods we serve. He must be the only One. We are surrounded, like the Israelites of ancient times, by other religions and idols. We need to be strong and not succumb to other gods.

Worship God Alone

"You shall not make for yourself an image
in the form of anything in heaven above or on
the earth beneath or in the waters below. You shall not
bow down to them or worship them; for I, the
Lord your God, am a jealous God." Exodus 20:4-5

This commandment is strongly connected to the first one. It was not at all unusual in biblical times to worship many gods. God's command is thus: I am the only true God; you shall not bow down to other gods.

Today we don't have statuettes or tree stumps that we bow to; the idols in our lives are different. Today's idols can often be seen as our work, possessions, sports, even our children. It is basically anything that is more important than our relationship with God. Do you put your hope in material possessions? Then money is your god. It is easy to worship other things rather than God. Society has changed to such an extent that it seems just fine to put your trust and hope in worldly things rather than in God. Examine your life and see if there are any idols or gods besides the Lord.

God's Name Is Holy

"You shall not misuse the name of the LORD your God, for the LORD will not hold anyone guiltless who misuses His name." Exodus 20:7

God is holy and His Name is holy. Because we respect God, we mustn't use His Name as an expletive when we get a fright or are surprised.

It is unsettling to see how people use God's name in vain today. In movies and TV shows it has become so common that some people don't even hear it anymore. And many people don't even regard it as swearing. Does this bother you? Do Christians not implicitly give consent to people to use God's name in vain by their silence?

Is it not time to stand up and say, "No, I'm switching off the TV. I'm not watching this movie"? You're not overreacting if it offends you when people misuse the Lord's name. You love God and therefore want to obey His commands.

Keep the Day of Rest

"Remember the Sabbath day by keeping it holy.
Six days you shall labor and do all your work,
but the seventh day is a Sabbath to the LORD your
God. On it you shall not do any work." Exodus 20:8-10

God created the earth and everything in it in six days, and on the seventh day He rested. He blessed the seventh day and set it apart as His holy day.

The Lord didn't stop His work on the seventh day because He was tired and needed to rest. No, He set the day apart so people may rest like He rested. It is not a command to do nothing – it is a day to rest in Him.

Deuteronomy explains further why we need to rest on the Sabbath – so that we can remember the great things God has done in the past: "Remember that you were slaves in Egypt and that the LORD your God brought you out of there with a mighty hand and an outstretched arm. Therefore the LORD your God has commanded you to observe the Sabbath day" (Deuteronomy 5:15). Use this day of rest that God gave you to grow in Him and move closer to Him.

Respect Your Parents

"Honor your father and your mother, so that you may live long in the land the LORD your God is giving you." Exodus 20:12

This command is the only one with a promise: If you honor your mother and father, you will have a long life in the land the Lord gives you. Like we respect our heavenly Father, we must also respect our earthly parents. Then we will be rewarded.

Many things are wrong in the world today. It is as if society has fallen into complete disrespect. People don't care about each other anymore. You put yourself first and that's that. Are the roots of this not found in the family setting? Many children today don't have any respect for their parents. One sees it in shopping malls, restaurants, at school events.

Is it not time for parents to apply their God-given authority in their homes? A child who respects his father today will respect his fellow man tomorrow. How are things in your home? Does it encourage respect for others?

You Shall Not Murder

"You shall not murder." Exodus 20:13

Well, it's obvious, right? Like we've seen, God's commandments keep us safe. God is in control of life and with this command He protects us from each other. In ancient times, though, life was not worth much.

Most people don't seriously consider killing someone, but don't feel good if you're one of them. Listen to what Jesus says in Matthew 5:21-22: "You have heard that it was said to the people long ago, 'You shall not murder, and anyone who murders will be subject to judgment.' But I tell you that anyone who is angry with a brother or sister will be subject to judgment."

What Jesus was saying is that we easily commit murder in our hearts when we're angry at someone. Examine your heart and make sure you're not subject to judgment.

Stay True to Each Other

"You shall not commit adultery." Exodus 20:14

Together with not using the Lord's name in vain, this command is equally watered-down today.

Marriage is holy, and when two people get married, they become one before God. Sadly, it happens so often that our love for each other wanes after a few years. People are eager to make excuses: "We drifted apart", "The children kept us busy", "He was always working."

The truth is that there is no excuse for a roving eye or heart. If you've made a promise before God, you can't allow anyone to put this relationship in jeopardy.

If you've betrayed your marriage vows – end the relationship, even if it seems innocent. Don't be tempted to justify your actions by comments like: "She made me feel special" or "He treated me like a queen." Always be true to your spouse.

Do Not Steal

"You shall not steal." Exodus 20:15

If you think about yourself, you don't think that you're a thief, right? This command is actually about more than robbing a bank or shoplifting.

Many of us steal without realizing it. If you're always late for work or not productive, you're stealing from your employer. You're stealing time and money, because you get paid for work you're not delivering.

Are you cheating on an insurance claim? Then you're stealing from the institution involved, because you're receiving money that you never really lost.

It may seem innocent at that particular moment, but don't be tempted to be dishonest in receiving things you don't actually deserve.

Don't Lie

"You shall not give false testimony against your neighbor." Exodus 20:16

In ancient times it was very important to give a true testimony, because your testimony could prove someone's innocence or guilt. Today we have all sorts of forensic experts who do the same. Still, the command to be honest hasn't changed.

Honesty is an indication of someone's integrity. When someone always twists or adapts the truth, before long no one believes them, even if they think they're not getting caught. We must always speak the truth, even when it's difficult.

Think about the times when someone lied to you and how hard it was to trust that person again. Lies destroy relationships and alienate people. The answer is simple: Don't lie. You can perhaps lie to people, but God knows the truth.

Stick to the truth – it makes things so much easier for yourself, and it's a command from God.

Jealousy

"You shall not covet your neighbor's house. You shall not covet your neighbor's wife, or his male or female servant, his ox or donkey, or anything that belongs to your neighbor." Exodus 20:17

One almost wonders why this is part of the Ten Commandments. We all desire things we don't have: a new car, a bigger house, or a better job. In actual fact, it's not so innocent to desire things we don't have.

The danger is where these desires could lead. Some people are so consumed by jealousy that they do things that are not in line with a Christian life. Some people even turn to crime to get what they want. Whether it's stealing money to buy something you desire or just taking something that doesn't belong to you, it is still wrong.

Some people can be blinded by their jealousy and as a result don't see the gifts they receive. This command tells us to be thankful for the wonderful gifts God has given each of us.

God's Hand Protects Us

"Showing love to a thousand generations of those who love Me and keep My commandments." Exodus 20:6

What a wonderful thought! God gave us the Ten Commandments to uphold order in society and to keep us safe. The first two commandments were given to us to ensure that we worship no other god besides the Lord.

We've seen that most of the commandments are not even difficult to obey – they are obvious and logical things to do to keep us safe and happy. But listen to what God is saying about people who obey His commandments: He will show His love to a thousand generations. It's almost too great to fathom. Some of us can trace our family tree back three or four generations, but thousands?

Do you understand that your obedience can be beneficial to your children and their children's children and their children? Is there a better way to show them love than by dedicating them, albeit indirectly, to God?

Whom Do You Trust?

I trust in You, LORD; I say,
"You are my God." Psalm 31:14

Your first instinct is perhaps to say, "I trust in God." It is what we've been taught, not so? We must trust God in all things.

But think about it. What is your first reaction in a crisis? Do you go to God immediately, or is God often the last resort, when nothing else has worked? What do you do amidst a financial crisis: Do you go to your bank manager or to God? Have you ever thought of giving your financial problems to God?

I'm not saying you should sit back and take no responsibility; what you should do is ask God for the necessary wisdom to make the right financial decisions. Ask Him to make you content with what you have so that you don't fall into the debt trap. Always go to God first, and let Him guide your life.

Stand Up for God

I will always obey Your law, for ever and ever. Your decrees are the theme of my song wherever I lodge. This has been my practice: I obey Your precepts. The law from Your mouth is more precious to me than thousands of pieces of silver and gold. Psalm 119:44, 54, 56, 72

In other religions you don't dare say anything against their god. They will reprimand you and they're even prepared to die for it. They are passionate about protecting their god. Are we Christians the same? Not always. How many Christians are prepared to stand up for the truth? Forget about dying for the truth! Aren't we happy just to keep quiet? To say nothing in order to keep the peace? God doesn't need us to protect Him, but we disappoint Him when we keep quiet when we should speak up. Aren't we betraying Him when people use His name in vain and we say nothing?

We must stop having so little faith. When you stand up for God, He will never leave you or forsake you. He will strengthen you and give you the right words. You simply need to trust Him.

NOVEMBER

Learn from Jesus

"Come to Me, all you who are weary and burdened, and I will give you rest." Matthew 11:28

Jesus invites us in Matthew to come to Him with all our burdens and problems. Jesus is concerned about our emotional and physical well-being. With these words He's actually asking how we are doing.

We live in a hurried society, which sets huge demands on us, whether it's at work and the hours in the day are not enough, or at home where the demands of your spouse or children are simply overwhelming.

Jesus invites all of us to lay the things that leave us tired and burdened at His feet. We can only find rest for our souls with Him. He is our rest. We must just remember not to pick our burdens up again once we've left them with Jesus. We must leave them there. It's not necessary to feel weary and tired all the time – find your rest in Jesus.

What Jesus Has Done

How can we thank God enough? 1 Thessalonians 3:9

Even the most perfect, pious people are not without sin. We are all sinners and we need a Savior.

Fortunately, Jesus came to earth and broke the hold that the devil has on our lives. He died for our sins on the cross. Think about it carefully: Christ came to earth and paid the price for your sins with His life. You don't have to bear the burden, because He carried it for you.

The question now is: How do you live in answer to this? Do you carry on living as before, or is your whole life a song of thanksgiving to God for your salvation? We can't just live our lives the way we want to. We must be grateful for what He's done for us. We must live Jesus' love every day and share the wonderful gifts from His hand with others.

Strong in the Lord

No temptation has overtaken you except what is common to mankind. And God is faithful; He will not let you be tempted beyond what you can bear. But when you are tempted, He will also provide a way out so that you can endure it. 1 Corinthians 10:13

It has become common practice today to do something wrong and just declare, "It's the devil's fault." Yes, it probably is the devil's fault, but it's also your fault because you didn't resist the temptation.

We read in 1 Corinthians that when temptations come, God will provide a way out. Here's the catch: You must stand strong. You must pray earnestly to the Father to protect you and strengthen you so you will be able to resist temptation.

You can't just give in and blame the devil. When it feels like you're being tempted, pray and ask for strength. Remember, each time you stand strong and resist temptation you'll be stronger the next time.

Get to Know the Will of God

Now these things occurred as examples to keep us from setting our hearts on evil things as they did. 1 Corinthians 10:6

While Israel was enslaved in Egypt they begged God to free them. We know the story of how God sent ten plagues, and how they crossed the Red Sea on dry ground. He also guided them by day and by night.

The Israelites, however, didn't know God, and instead of being taught by Him and getting to know Him better, they rebelled against God and regretted being freed from Egypt. The result was that the people died in the desert and never entered the Promised Land.

Most of us also act like the Israelites. We see God's miracles, we experience His power in our lives, but when we're required to live in a relationship with Him, we complain. Don't follow the example of the Israelites and die in the desert without seeing the Promised Land.

A Promised Land for All

God looked on the Israelites and was concerned about them. Exodus 2:25

Just like God's people were saved from Egypt, He can save you from whatever is keeping you captive. We read in Exodus that God saw their groaning and was concerned about His people. He also sees your needs and is concerned about you.

Think about it: God hears the groanings and calls for help from His people and He saves them, even people who don't have a real relationship with Him. There's nothing left to make you think God doesn't hear your calls for help. You're His child. Be assured that God wants to help you and He hears you.

He wants to lead each of us to our own Promised Land. A place of fulfillment, meaning, purpose, intimacy and knowledge of God – a life of purpose and meaning.

Enter the Promised Land

The LORD said to Moses, "This is the land I promised on oath to Abraham, Isaac and Jacob when I said, 'I will give it to your descendants.' I have let you see it with your eyes, but you will not cross over into it." Deuteronomy 34:4

Some of the Israelites died in Egypt and the rest died in the desert. Only Joshua and Caleb were allowed to enter the Promised Land. And because of his disobedience, not even Moses was allowed to enter.

I don't know about you, but this moves me. I don't want to die in the desert or in Egypt. I'm one of those people who believe that if there is a small group, I'll be one of them. I want to be one of the people who leave the desert behind, enter the Promised Land and receive everything God has promised.

Do you want to enter the Promised Land? Do you want to be one of the few who endure to the end? Work at your relationship with God and obey Him.

Your Promised Land

Hear, Israel, and be careful to obey so that it may go well with you and that you may increase greatly in a land flowing with milk and honey. Deuteronomy 6:3

What is your Promised Land? Is it what God has planned for you, or is it your own dreams and plans?

We read in the Scriptures that when God created us, He gave meaning to our lives and made us with a unique purpose in life. Why did God make us so unique? Because our Promised Land is inside us. It resembles our dreams and goals in life. We're here for a specific purpose.

We were born for something great, but we must listen to God's voice. He guides our paths and wants to help us reach our goal and purpose in life. Be obedient and follow Him. Allow Him to direct your footsteps so that you can enter your Promised Land.

Your Purpose in Life

The body is not made up of one part but of many. 1 Corinthians 12:14

What is your purpose in life? Why are you here? What must you do?

All of us have a role to play in the world. Some people seem to have more glamorous and important roles to fulfill, while others seem to have less important ones. But we read in the Bible that one role is not more important than another. You can't decide that your role in life is insignificant. God needs everyone, and each person's function is important.

God created everybody equal, and no one is more important than another. Believe in yourself like God believes in you, and don't underestimate your potential. You have a purpose in life. It just sometimes takes a bit of effort to find out what it is.

Temporary Enjoyment

I observed everything going on under the sun, and really, it is all meaningless – like chasing after the wind. Ecclesiastes 1:14 NLT

We know that God has a purpose and plan for our lives. Many of us are, however, battling to find out what it is. Let me give you a simple answer: It has to do with eternity.

Many of the things we do are temporary. It's here today and gone tomorrow. It gives temporary enjoyment, temporary fulfillment. These are things like money, earthly possessions and jewels. We chase after things that only give temporary joy and happiness. We often forget that we must work with eternity in mind.

It's not wrong to work hard, earn money and buy nice things. But if this is all that defines our lives, it's a chasing after the wind. We must find things to do that have eternal value. Ask the Father in prayer to reveal things to you of eternal value.

Do What Really Matters

Do your best to present yourself to God as one approved, a worker who does not need to be ashamed and who correctly handles the word of truth. 2 Timothy 2:15

Let's discuss things of eternal value. Do you know what they are? Let me give you a few examples.

Parents, the way you raise your child has eternal value. When you pray with your child or teach them about Jesus, you're doing something of eternal value. I've heard countless stories of people who are most happy when they do something for someone else.

A successful young man told me that the best times in his life are when he has a trunk filled with blankets and food to give to the needy. Another man told me that he is most happy when he is helping out at an orphanage.

When you look away from yourself, give up your selfish needs and focus on others, then you're busy doing things that will matter in eternity.

Are You Happy?

Whoever looks intently into the perfect law that gives freedom, and continues in it – not forgetting what they have heard, but doing it – they will be blessed in what they do. James 1:25

How happy are you today? Is your life fulfilled? When your children describe you, what do they say? "Daddy is happy"? "Mom shines"? Or do they say with a frown, "Dad is hot-tempered" or "Mom doesn't smile a lot"?

How happy are you today? What do you enjoy in life? For some people joy is found in giving things away to those who are underprivileged. To others it is giving of themselves and their time.

We read in the Bible that we'll be blessed when we study the law and live according to it. When we live our lives according to God's perfect law, we'll automatically care for others. Our focus will shift from ourselves to others. Their happiness becomes ours. Try it!

Find Your Own Calcutta

Each of you should use whatever gift you have received to serve others, as faithful stewards of God's grace in its various forms. 1 Peter 4:10

I've recently read Mother Teresa's autobiography. She lived for Christ and for her fellow humans. This was her only goal and purpose in life.

She didn't have many earthly treasures, but her heavenly riches awaited her in heaven. We are often scared of giving things away to others. We believe the devil's lies that we need earthly treasures to be happy. As a result we continue to be unfulfilled.

You find meaning in life when you care for others and when you serve them. You don't have to be Mother Teresa and work in the streets of Calcutta. But we can, like she once wrote to a boy, find our own Calcutta. There are people in need everywhere. We must just be willing to see it. We have received so many gifts of the Spirit; we must use them and share them with others.

Wholehearted Service

We are God's handiwork, created in Christ Jesus to do good works, which God prepared in advance for us to do. Ephesians 2:10

Why are only a few people willing to reach out to others? It is after all a biblical commission. The answer is easy: We are controlled by fear.

People are afraid to serve God wholeheartedly, because of what will become of their own lives. We believe the devil's lies – that we'll lose everything when we put others first. We believe that if we live fully for God, we'll be unhappy, lonely and poor. The devil makes us believe that we need to care for ourselves, because no one else will. We forget about our Father who owns everything in heaven and on earth.

Can we really believe that He won't care for us? We can't honestly think that He'll leave us to our own devices.

It's easy: God expects us to dedicate our lives to doing good. And if we're obedient, He will care for us. It's a biblical fact.

A Clean Fountain

Like a muddied spring or a polluted well are the righteous who give way to the wicked. Proverbs 25:26

What we allow into our thoughts and minds is expressed in our actions and deeds. Evil thoughts lead to evil deeds. Fortunately the contrary is also true: Good thoughts lead to good deeds.

We must be very careful of worldly influences. It's easy to allow all kinds of wrong things to enter our thoughts. Before we know it, our thoughts are polluted. When this happens we don't see the beauty of life, our fellow humans or even God anymore. Worst of all, we start acting according to the realities created in our thoughts, realities that are often far removed from the truth.

Be cautious about what you allow into your mind. Open yourself up to God's Word and the beauty in life. It will become evident in your actions. Be a sparkling fountain.

Be There for Others

Religion that God our Father accepts
as pure and faultless is this: to look after
orphans and widows in their distress. James 1:27

Most people have more gifts than they would admit. We often look at what others have with ungrateful hearts. When we've convinced ourselves that we don't have enough, we don't give so freely to others.

Maybe it's time to start looking at people who have less than us. The Bible talks about orphans and widows, and today there is so much need in so many forms. You demonstrate your love for God through the way you are prepared to help people in need.

You've received so much from God's hand, so share it with people who are less fortunate. Share because you're grateful for your own gifts that you've received so undeservedly. Ask God to show you today where you can help someone in need.

Always Tell the Truth

Jesus said, "All you need to say is simply 'Yes' or 'No'; anything beyond this comes from the evil one." Matthew 5:37

Jesus couldn't put it clearer. Let your "Yes" be "Yes" and your "No" be "No", nothing more and nothing less. Be reliable and honest in all things.

We sometimes think that honesty is not lying. Your "Yes" is your "Yes." But honesty entails so much more than telling the truth. It also involves putting all the facts on the table and not leaving anything out. If you tell a half-truth or give incomplete information, you're lying.

Even though you think people don't know it, God knows. You can't hide anything from Him, and with your half-truths and lies you disappoint Him. Be someone whom others can trust. You don't want to be known as someone who doesn't stick to the truth, right? Always tell the whole truth – your heavenly Father wants nothing less.

Peace vs. Revenge

Do not repay anyone evil for evil. Be careful to do what is right in the eyes of everyone. If it is possible, as far as it depends on you, live at peace with everyone. Romans 12:17-18

Paul wrote this letter to the believers in Rome to tell them of the gospel. And, like everything in the Bible, this still applies today.

What Paul means with this command is that we shouldn't allow evil to rule over good. If you take revenge, evil wins. It is often only human to want to take revenge, but don't allow sin to rule in your heart. If you live at peace with all people you will be able to stand before God with a pure and clean heart.

We often forget that our actions reflect our love for God. If you want revenge all the time and make plans to bring about someone's downfall, you're actually saying that God is not a God of love, but a God of revenge and punishment. Examine your heart and ask God to remove the vengeance you harbor. Live in such a way that others can see God's love. Leave the retribution to Him.

Be a Good Example

Live such good lives among the pagans
that, though they accuse you of doing wrong,
they may see your good deeds and glorify
God on the day He visits us. 1 Peter 2:12

We as Christians must never forget that we're living under a magnifying glass. In a world that has become increasingly intolerant towards Christians, it's important to live in such a way so that no one can throw a stone at us.

Wherever Christians find themselves, they should live blameless lives. What exactly does that mean for us? Be honest, don't lie and cheat, watch your language, live morally and keep the Ten Commandments. Let anything that unbelievers or hostile people say be mere lies.

It's not always an easy task – unfortunately, Christians have to face the same temptations as unbelievers. We must, however, act in such a way that the world will see God's presence in our lives. And who knows: You might save souls for God through your example. What a wonderful thought!

Someone to Look Up To

As for you, continue in what you have learned and have become convinced of, because you know those from whom you learned it. 2 Timothy 3:14

A mentor is someone who gives wise counsel, an expert in their field, a confidant, a teacher. In short, it's someone to look up to and to learn from.

Most people have mentors in life. You might not realize it, but there is someone who has made an impact on you. A mentor needn't be a successful business person. It can be someone who stands in a close and sincere relationship with the Father. And that's perhaps the best mentor – someone who can teach us more of the Bible, someone whose relationship with the Father inspires us.

Be wise when choosing a mentor. Choose someone who can lead you to a more intimate relationship with the Father, not someone who'll lead you to the world.

We've Received His Grace

For it is by grace you have been saved,
through faith – and this is not from
yourselves, it is the gift of God. Ephesians 2:8

For many Christians the word *grace* is too familiar. We have received grace, we were saved by grace, and God is gracious towards us. But do we realize what this word really means? Aren't we making it shallow and common by our free use of the idea of grace?

Grace is something we don't deserve; in fact, grace can almost be seen as the opposite of fairness and righteousness. Because of grace we don't receive the punishment for our sins that we actually deserve. We mustn't take grace lightly. Grace cost Jesus His life.

Let us be thankful every day and let our gratitude be revealed through our actions. Without God's grace we would be condemned for eternity. Thank God every day for His wonderful gift of grace and live deserving of this grace.

Quiet in God's Presence

Grow in the grace and knowledge of our Lord and Savior Jesus Christ. To Him be glory both now and forever! Amen. 2 Peter 3:18

How can we improve our relationship with the Father today? The answer is simple: We must become still before Him.

Christians don't always realize the importance of being quiet in His presence. When we become quiet at God's feet through prayer and Bible study, we get to know Him better. And when we get to know Him better, we discover His will for our lives. We discover how we as Christians ought to live and what's expected from us. We live in a broken world and without God's guidance we'll simply be overwhelmed by our burdens.

Quiet time also helps us to focus on the spiritual realm. It's where God is and where He moves. It's the world where your life is written in the Book of Life, and where you'll spend eternity.

Build Your Relationship

"Great and marvelous are Your deeds, Lord God Almighty. Just and true are Your ways, King of the nations." Revelation 15:3

As modern people we are sometimes tempted to think that we don't need God anymore. Thanks to technology, few things are impossible.

More than ever we need to become still before God and get to know Him. We must make an effort to build our relationship with Him. Then we can know and understand His will. We're tempted to rush our relationship with God. God must just help us "quickly." He must "quickly" fix what we've messed up. He must "quickly" provide this or that.

When things don't happen our way, we can't imagine that the fault lies with us. God is great and His deeds are too wonderful for words, but we miss them because we don't have a true relationship with Him.

Become still before God today and build your relationship with Him. If you get to know Him intimately, you'll be able to see His greatness.

Saved by Christ

He has saved us and called us to a holy life – not because of anything we have done but because of His own purpose and grace. This grace was given us in Christ Jesus. 2 Timothy 1:9

You can only have a relationship with God because of what Jesus did for you on the cross. God decided even before creation to give us His grace.

This He did through Jesus Christ. We are chosen, called and saved to live lives dedicated to the honor and glory of God. Imagine someone living a dedicated life, someone in a relationship with the Father, someone who prays and who knows God. You are chosen for such a life. Even before creation God knew that Jesus would come to earth to bridge the gap between God and people so that we could have an intimate relationship with Him.

We are created and called to have a relationship with God. You were created to be still at the Father's feet. Be still today and learn from Him.

Don't Neglect Quiet Time

Look to the LORD and His strength;
seek His face always. 1 Chronicles 16:11

I know there are people who think this is not for them. They feel they don't have time, or they're too ordinary for something like *lectio divina*.

It's a mistake to think like this. You and I were made for quiet times with God and your relationship with Him is the most important one. Like a fish was made to live in water, we were made to have a relationship with God.

What happens when you take a fish out of the water? It dies. Remove yourself from the presence of God and you'll die. You are made to meditate – it's your food, your life, your breath. If you stop, your body will live, but your soul will die. Then everything becomes a chasing after the wind and nothing makes sense; everything is empty because you are a fish and you are made for water.

Prayer Involves Listening

Pray continually. 1 Thessalonians 5:17

We often make the mistake of thinking that prayer is a one-way conversation from our side. Prayer is also being quiet and listening to what God wants to tell us.

Ages ago the church fathers spent hours in God's presence. They stayed in isolation and prayer, mediated on the Scriptures and got to know God. This way of becoming quiet before God is called *lectio divina*. The sole purpose of lectio divina is to hear the Lord's voice. It literally means "divine reading." The church fathers didn't rush their time with God; they sat peacefully and quietly in His presence and got to know His will.

The command in 1 Thessalonians is not merely an instruction to pray, but also to become quiet before God and to hear His voice.

Let God Teach You

I saw the Lord always before me. Because He is at my right hand, I will not be shaken. Therefore my heart is glad and my tongue rejoices; my body also will rest in hope, because You will not abandon me to the realm of the dead. Acts 2:25-27

We've seen that even before creation it was ordained that we were created to live in a relationship with God.

It's not complicated. Go to your room and dedicate yourself to the Lord. Read your Bible until a certain passage speaks to your heart. Meditate on it, write it down and find out what you need to do with this knowledge. Let the Scriptures speak to you and talk to God about what you've read. Ask Him for the necessary knowledge and wisdom to understand what you've read and apply it to your life.

Say for instance you read "flee from sin." Ask the Lord to show you any sin in your life. Take note of it and stop it. You can only learn when you become quiet before the Lord.

A Thankful Heart

Devote yourselves to prayer, being watchful and thankful. Colossians 4:2

The next step in order to grow closer to God is to have a thankful heart. What happens then? Thanking Him comes naturally.

You thank God for being able to speak with Him, that your day will look different, for being able to be in a relationship with Him, for being able to pray. Thank Him, thank Him, thank Him. Suddenly you get an attitude of thanksgiving.

You see, when you follow the right steps and you reach thankfulness, it becomes easy. Then your eyes change and you see life differently. You see your family, spouse, children, work and the whole world differently because you're filled with gratitude.

Start giving thanks to God today for what you've received from Him.

Learn to Be Thankful

I will sacrifice a thank offering to You and call on the name of the LORD. Psalm 116:17

Even if it comes easily, thankfulness is something you learn to do. You can't accept everything as obvious. You can't think that everything you have, you deserve.

When you learn to live a thankful life every day, your first step will be a deeper and more intimate relationship with Lord. Start by giving thanks for everything in your life, and praise God.

Learn to be thankful for everything He gives us and does for us: oxygen, rain, birds, you name it. Then you can start living thankfully.

The result? Praise! When you're thankful, you can't but sing God's praises for your gifts and for His care.

Praise and Worship

"Sacrifice thank offerings to God, fulfill your vows to the Most High. Those who sacrifice thank offerings honor Me, and to the blameless I will show My salvation." Psalm 50:14, 23

Praise and worship on a Sunday shouldn't be the only time during your week when you thank God for His goodness. No, this time of singing together should be the close of a week's worth of praise and worship.

You must praise and worship God every day – at home, at work, in the car. You can't just sing in church on Sunday without singing during the week. You can't be cold and distant the whole week and think everything will be OK after you've sung a few songs to Him on a Sunday.

Praise and worship must happen every day of the week. You must live with a heart filled with gratitude every day for what He has given you. Praise and worship on a Sunday should be the highlight of a week lived in gratitude to God.

Church Is Important

Not giving up meeting together, as some are in the habit of doing, but encouraging one another – and all the more as you see the Day approaching. Hebrews 10:25

We live rushed lives. Sometimes we don't even have five minutes to ourselves. Even our weekends are jam-packed with activities.

We are then tempted to stay at home on Sundays rather than to go to church. We often have "noble" excuses, such as spending time with our children or parents. We just want to relax a bit.

This is where we make the mistake. We often read in the Bible that we shouldn't stay away from meeting together with other believers. It's important to hear a spiritual message on a Sunday. It's important to meet together with other believers. We must praise and worship the Lord together. It's good for our souls to go to church every Sunday and receive a message from God. Don't give in to the temptation of not going to church.

DECEMBER

The Angels Worshiped Him

They were calling to one another: "Holy, holy, holy is the LORD Almighty; the whole earth is full of His glory." Isaiah 6:3

Our God is a mighty and holy God. He is our God, the great I Am. Even the angels bowed before His throne in worship.

How do you praise and worship God? Do you fall down in reverence before Him and worship Him, or is He just Someone who must fulfill your needs? We can only approach God in prayer when we – like the angels in heaven – acknowledge His might. Only when we sing of His greatness and holiness can we come to Him with our long list of requests. We are created to glorify God and this we need to do. Unbelievers must see through our actions that He is omnipotent. We cannot deal with God halfheartedly and expect Him to bless us.

Examine your heart and the way you worship God. Can others see how great your God is through the way you worship?

Be Thankful

Since we are receiving a kingdom that cannot be shaken, let us be thankful, and so worship God acceptably with reverence and awe. Hebrews 12:28

By being thankful you're taking your first steps toward a deeper relationship with God. Does it feel like praise and worship are overflowing in your heart and you can't contain it? Then you're on the right track.

Think about it this way: if you do something for someone and they don't thank you, would you be eager to do something for them again? No, not really. How about if they thank you over and over? You'd be more willing to do something for them the next time, right?

If you think the Lord is not doing much for you, look at the way you thank Him. Do you take things for granted and not thank God enough? God gives good things to you from His gracious hand, but not because you deserve it. He already gave His Son – that's more than enough. Start thanking Him for all the wonderful gifts that He so undeservedly bestows on you.

Praying for Yourself

My God, whom I praise, do not remain silent. Psalm 109:1

Many of our prayers are for our loved ones and for ourselves. However, we should not merely pray and think all the responsibility now lies with God. We must do our part.

Say for instance you pray every morning, "O God, please protect my children today." However, you drive like a maniac and put your own life in danger, or you allow your toddler to sit in the front seat while you drive at high speed on the freeway. Where is your responsibility to yourself and your children? You can't pray for protection but act irresponsibly.

You can't ask for purity but at the same time lie and cheat. How can God make you pure if you contaminate your heart with lies? God wants to protect us and make us pure, but we must do our part and live responsibly.

God Wants to Hear You

Do not be anxious about anything, but in every situation, by prayer and petition, with thanksgiving, present your requests to God. Philippians 4:6

In Philippians, God invites us to come to Him in prayer. It doesn't mean that you can throw everything down at His feet and He'll fix it. God says we must talk to Him about it. And what will He do? He will speak to you. However, you can't shift all the responsibility over to Him. God will tell you to do a few things yourself first.

We often think we've prayed about a topic and then it's over and done with. But when we go to Him with everything – like God asks us to – He will speak to us. We must listen to His voice because He will often give us the answers. It remains our responsibility to apply what He said to our lives.

Next time you go to God with a load of requests and problems, stay a little while longer. Wait for the answers, listen for His guidance and then go out and do it.

Proclaim the Gospel

Jesus said, "Peace be with you! As the Father has sent Me, I am sending you." John 20:21

Jesus gives us the command to go out and spread the gospel. For some people this is a difficult task. It is understandable, because not everyone is a public speaker. It's not easy for all people to witness about their faith. Few people really feel called to go to a foreign land and do missionary work.

Still, you can witness – with your life. Can people see God's presence in your life? Often your actions speak much louder than your words.

Others can see Jesus when you live an honorable life, when you're honest and hardworking, when you treat others fairly. They can see Him when your face shines with joy because of all your blessings in life. Look at your life: Is it a worthy sermon to those who do not know God?

Money and Possessions

Though your riches increase, do not set your heart on them. Psalm 62:10

People today are much wealthier than in biblical times. We have a lot more possessions; the psalmist's warning is therefore meant for our ears today.

Money is important – we can't get away from that. You need money to survive; to put food on the table for your family and clothes on their backs. Still, money mustn't become an idol in your life. It shouldn't become such a dominant force in your life that you're willing to do anything to get more of it.

Don't ever forget that money can't save you, only God can. Work hard at your relationship with Him, because without God in your life you can have all the riches in the world, but you'll still have nothing.

Rejoice in Everyday Things

A cheerful heart is good medicine, but a crushed spirit dries up the bones. Proverbs 17:22

This is so true. Have you realized that you can face so much more when you're cheerful? And how life can seem like a giant mountain when you feel down?

God wants us to be cheerful. Take note, not in a frivolous and superficial manner. Cheerful people rejoice in everyday things. They rejoice about the good things in their lives, and it's enjoyable being around them.

Life is perhaps not always a joyful song, but there must be something to rejoice about, not so? If you think that you have nothing to rejoice about, look carefully at your life and find one thing to be glad about.

Later you'll realize that it will become easier to find things to be thankful for – the more you focus on the good things, the clearer they will become in your life.

Pray for the Right Things

You do not have because you do not ask God. James 4:2

Short and sweet, right? However, we must not misinterpret this Scripture verse. We mustn't think that we can pray for anything on earth and God will give it to us.

The next verse reads, "When you ask, you do not receive, because you ask with wrong motives, that you may spend what you get on your pleasures" (James 4:3). Prayer is not a personal wish list. We must first get to know God's will for our lives, and pray accordingly. Prayer and what we pray for must always be to God's glory.

When we have an intimate relationship with God, it becomes easier to put ourselves second and not pray for our own selfish ambitions.

What do you pray for? Do your prayers glorify God, or satisfy your own needs? Work on your relationship with God so that your prayers will glorify Him.

Examine Your Heart

Dear friends, if our hearts do not condemn us, we have confidence before God and receive from Him anything we ask, because we keep His commands and do what pleases Him. 1 John 3:21-22

We've all prayed for something and didn't receive it. *What's the use of praying, then?* many of us are tempted to wonder. We want to ask God why we are not getting what we asked for.

Perhaps we need to examine our hearts. God's command is to love His Son, and each other. When we're not obedient to His commands, we can't stand before Him with a clear conscience. We ask for our own selfish needs. Then we mustn't wonder why we don't receive what we pray for, because we're not asking for God's will in our lives.

If you continue to pray self-centered prayers, they will destroy your life. Obey His command and pray according to His will for your life.

Your Joy Is in God

Take delight in the LORD, and He will give you the desires of your heart. Psalm 37:4

Think about it quickly: What are the desires of your heart? A red Ferrari, a beach house, the perfect family, a big salary?

Read the words before the part "and He will give you the desires of your heart." What does it say? "Take delight in the Lord." We want to know why we don't receive the desires of our hearts. The answer is easy, and also unsettling: because our hearts are corrupt.

When you've found your joy in God and enjoy His presence and quality time with Him, your desires and heart will also change. Your desire then becomes the conversion and salvation of other people. You want to become a person full of love and grace, delighting in the Lord.

Then you will receive the desires of your heart, because your desires will be in line with God's will for your life.

Pray for Others First

I urge, then, first of all, that petitions, prayers, intercession and thanksgiving be made for all people. 1 Timothy 2:1

We can't accuse God of not listening to our prayers. We must first change before we can pray sincerely.

Exactly what is 1 Timothy 2:1 saying to us? First of all, we must pray for all people. Let's be honest: What do we usually pray for first? We pray for ourselves. We first pray for our spouse and children and work and money and accounts. Here Paul teaches us that when it comes to praying, we must first have a heart for other people.

We also read that we should pray for our leaders and those in authority so that we can live quiet lives completely dedicated to God. Put yourself in second place for a change and pray for others first. Then you will see how your prayer life will change.

Make the World a Better Place

Confess your sins to each other and pray for each other so that you may be healed. The prayer of a righteous person is powerful and effective. James 5:16

What will you discover when you get to know God's heart better? You'll realize that He wants to save all people and that He wants to use you to help accomplish this.

The first place where He wants to use you to make the world a better place is in your quiet time. That's why our quiet times with God are so important. We can't just read one or two Scripture verses from the Bible and pray a quick prayer. God wants to speak to our hearts and minds in our quiet time.

He wants to change us so that our first thought is not ourselves anymore, but our fellow men. Our first thought should be: *Lord, all I ask is for You to use me to do Your will. Who must I pray for? For whom must I intercede? Where can I go today in line with Your will? What do You want me to do?* And that's how the world can change: by changing yourself first.

In Quietness and Trust

Be still before the Lord and wait patiently for Him; do not fret when people succeed in their ways, when they carry out their wicked schemes. Psalm 37:7

Part of our quiet time should involve being still before God. This involves a time of silence where we forget about our troubles and concerns and just focus on God. We rein our wandering thoughts in and just focus on our Almighty King and Creator of the universe. Instead of thinking about the fight you've just had, the mess the kids have made, what you're going to make for supper or how you are going to pay your bills – just be still before the Lord.

As you do so you will feel the cares of the day drain away and your fretting heart will calm down. You will realize once again that God is in control and that you need to simply trust Him and wait patiently for Him to help you. You will feel strengthened and encouraged to continue with your day. Always remember that, "In repentance and rest is your salvation, in quietness and trust is your strength" (Isaiah 30:15).

No Need to Fear

There is no fear in love. But perfect love drives out fear, because fear has to do with punishment. The one who fears is not made perfect in love. 1 John 4:18

It is supposed to be very simple: God loves us. He cares for us and protects us. Still, many people live in a state of paralyzing fear.

When we are constantly scared and afraid of everything, we're actually saying that we don't trust God to be good to us. We basically reject His promises. How would you feel if your children tell you they don't trust you to care for them? It would hurt you, right? Is that not what we're doing to the Father when we live fearful lives?

We have no reason to distrust our heavenly Father. Go to God today and ask Him to take away your fears. Ask Him to help you trust Him completely, and to believe when He says in the Bible that He will protect you.

Life Is Beautiful

Rejoice in the Lord always. I will say it again: Rejoice! Philippians 4:4

This is probably one of the most popular Scripture verses in the Bible. But how many of us live according to it? How many of us have made these words a part of our lives?

God is infinitely good to us and has given us many undeserved gifts; therefore we must rejoice. We must learn to always be glad, even when we don't feel like it. When we teach ourselves to see the beauty and good things in life, rejoicing will happen more easily. It's simple to spot people with a deep joy for life. They act differently, they experience negative things differently and it's just pleasant to be in their presence.

It is possible to always rejoice and be glad, it just takes a bit of practice. Find something right now to rejoice about.

Reconciliation between People

"Love your neighbor as yourself.
I am the LORD." Leviticus 19:18

In South Africa, December 16 is the Day of Reconciliation, a day to hold out a hand of peace, forgiveness and friendship.

Every country has issues concerning racism and tolerating differences. People don't always like each other, and here and there the hatred runs deep. We can all be a bit more tolerant towards people who are different from ourselves.

Most countries have different cultures, languages and races mixed into one. You don't have to be best friends with people you don't agree with, but at least be respectable and decent.

Try to understand someone else's viewpoint, and be less intense about your own. The fact is that we live in a certain country, and we must all work together to make a success of it. Reach out and build bridges of peace.

The Children in Our Lives

"Let the little children come to Me, and do not hinder them, for the kingdom of God belongs to such as these." Mark 10:14

Jesus didn't set children apart for nothing. Besides children being the hope of the future, they also give us – most of the time – so much joy.

You don't need to have your own to know how special children are. There is so much hope locked up inside them, and discovering the world anew with them is an experience that is so wonderful that it can almost not be put into words. We must look after and protect our children.

Whether you're an uncle, aunt, grandpa, grandma or just a close friend, protecting children should always be our highest priority. We live in a broken world and children are exposed to the most horrific things. Teach them to protect themselves when you're not there. Teach them to be vigilant – without being afraid of everything all the time. Dedicate them to God every day. We must give our best for our children. They're our hope and our future.

God's Love for Us

Dear friends, since God so loved us, we also ought to love one another. 1 John 4:11

In 1 John 4:7 we read that love comes from God and that everyone who loves is a child of God. God is love and He showed His love towards us by sending His own Son to the world so that we could live through Him.

Now, if God loved us so much that He was willing to send His Son, we ought to also love one another. One would think this is not a difficult task – we are after all Christians who experience God's love firsthand, right? Yet it's still difficult for some people.

If you struggle to love your neighbor, you need to make a purposeful effort to focus on the love that God has for us. The more your awareness of God's love grows, the more you'll experience how your love for your neighbor will grow.

Love Is More Than a Feeling

Let no debt remain outstanding, except the continuing debt to love one another, for whoever loves others has fulfilled the law. Romans 13:8

Love is not always about how you feel. The Bible says – and this is a command – that we must love each other. We are, however, sinful people, and often our love for others is seriously lacking.

Spouses who feel that they don't love each other anymore often receive the advice to treat each other as if they're still in love. The reasoning behind it is that if you act as if you love someone, it will later turn into real love. When we do this, the love eventually becomes more than just words. We'll find that we truly love one another.

Maybe we must also treat our fellow humans as if we already love them. Who knows, maybe one day we will discover that the "pretense" has turned into real love.

I Am Good Enough

Finally, brothers and sisters, whatever is true, whatever is noble, whatever is right, whatever is pure, whatever is lovely, whatever is admirable – if anything is excellent or praiseworthy – think about such things. Philippians 4:8

Our thoughts have a much greater influence on our lives than we realize. We become what we think and believe about ourselves.

It is true that it's much easier to think negative thoughts about ourselves – and believe them – than it is to think positive things.

We read in the Bible that we must think about things that are true, noble, right, pure, lovely and admirable. When we fill our thoughts with these praiseworthy things, there will not be any space left for negative thoughts.

Make a deliberate effort to see and believe only the good things in life and in yourself. You'll be amazed at the positive effect on your life.

God's Love in Us

Hope does not put us to shame, because God's love has been poured out into our hearts through the Holy Spirit, who has been given to us. Romans 5:5

What a wonderful thought: God's love is in us. He poured His love into our hearts through the Holy Spirit.

If we think about it carefully, it's almost too great to fathom. The great God who created the universe, who keeps everything in place and who sent His Son as an atonement for our sins – His love is in us.

We cannot – we dare not – keep this love to ourselves. It's love that urges us to reach out to our fellow man, to care for the less privileged, and to share His message of love and salvation with others. It is this love that encourages us to live lives of integrity.

It is His love that compels us to put Him first in all things. It is our Christian duty to go out and share His love with the world.

Extreme Love

We love because He first loved us. 1 John 4:19

Where does love begin? It starts with God who loves us. The responsibility to love, the ability, the gifts, the strength, the seed of love, the desire to love, is all inside us. The Bible is very clear on this command to love each other, and we have no excuse not to love.

The reason why we often don't love each other is because our hearts are closed to God's love. The moment our hearts are closed to love, God's love cannot flow through us to others. Open your heart today, not just to love others, but to receive God's love.

Remember, we all have the potential to show immense love, because God has poured His love into our hearts.

Let Kindness Rule

The Lord's servant must not be quarrelsome but must be kind to everyone, able to teach, not resentful. 2 Timothy 2:24

There is probably no one who can say with a clear conscience that they have never had an argument with anyone before. We are too human and too sinful.

We sometimes forget that we are God's ambassadors on earth. Christians often stand under a magnifying glass in a hostile world, and we can't afford to be quarrelsome. We read in the Bible that we are expected to be kind to everyone. It often requires a strong character to stand back and not retaliate. It doesn't mean that we're the punching bags of the world, but there are better ways to handle situations than to fight with everyone day after day.

Problems are better solved when you go to the person in peace and with constructive suggestions than to just start arguing. Ask the Lord for calmness of mind so that you don't become someone who fights all the time.

Christmas Eve

The Word became flesh and made
His dwelling among us. We have seen His glory,
the glory of the one and only Son, who came
from the Father, full of grace and truth. John 1:14

This time of year is a special time for Christians, when we celebrate the birth of our Savior and Redeemer. It is a time when "the Word became flesh and dwelt among us."

Despite busy shopping malls and lots of money spent during this time, it's as if there is a greater spirit of goodwill among people. Why would that be? Are we mesmerized by the Christmas lights and cheerful music, forgetting that we should celebrate Jesus' birth in our hearts every day of the year?

Christmas should not be a once-a-year occasion. We are to celebrate Jesus becoming human every day. We must live with a spirit of goodwill every day of the year and live out this goodwill, treating others in such a way that they see Jesus in our hearts.

Christmas in Your Heart

To us a Child is born, to us a Son is given,
and the government will be on His shoulders.
And He will be called Wonderful Counselor, Mighty
God, Everlasting Father, Prince of Peace. Isaiah 9:6

Many people give gifts on this day and share the day with loved ones. It's a day of being together. We must, however, not forget the real reason behind the celebrations.

Jesus was born for us; He came to take away our sins and to save us from eternal death. We must celebrate this day – Jesus becoming flesh for us. We must celebrate the fact that our Savior lives and sits on His throne and rules over His kingdom. Our festivities mustn't be superficial like the rest of the world, when tomorrow comes, don't forget about today's wonderful Gift.

It is important to receive the gift of God in your heart each day so that Christmas will be in your heart every day of the year.

Forgive Each Other

"Lord, how many times shall I forgive my brother or sister who sins against me? Up to seven times?" Matthew 18:21

We all know Jesus' answer to Peter's question about forgiveness: "I tell you, not seven times, but seventy-seven times" (Matthew 18:22).

However difficult it may seem, we must forgive each other time after time. It is difficult to forgive when it seems like we're the only ones doing the forgiving. The rest of the people just carry on, doing what they want without remorse or regret. But Jesus says we must even forgive seventy-seven times, because that's how many times we have been forgiven. We can't deny someone something that we ourselves have received.

Our forgiveness of others flows from our gratitude for the forgiveness we've received from God, and from others.

A Beautiful Sound

If I speak in the tongues of men or of angels, but do not have love, I am only a resounding gong or a clanging cymbal. 1 Corinthians 13:1

What is this Scripture verse really saying to us? It comes down to the fact that nothing in life matters if we don't have love. It tells us that if we do things without love, it's equivalent to just making a noise.

If there is no love in our hearts, it doesn't matter how many good and wonderful things we do, it means nothing.

Love gives meaning to our actions. Others can't see into our hearts, and sometimes it's easy to fool people. But we can't fool God – He sees our hearts. You don't want to make noise in God's ears, right?

Everything in life must happen from a foundation of love. Ask God to cleanse your heart and to fill it with love. Your deeds will mean so much more if you are motivated by love.

Who Is the Church?

Just as a body, though one, has many parts, but all its many parts form one body, so it is with Christ. 1 Corinthians 12:12

People go to church on Sundays and expect a biblical message for the week. This message must encourage them, increase their faith and strengthen them for the week ahead. For many people it's an hour of passive listening.

What many people don't realize is that they're also the church. You are the church when people see by the way you live that Christ lives in you. You are the church when you encourage and support someone. You are the church when you tell people of Christ's love and mercy, and lead them to salvation.

"Church" is not just a place we go to on a Sunday. It's not just a building that's empty for six days of the week. Church is the way we treat others and how we live out our faith. Church is our relationship with each other and our willingness to witness for Christ.

Your Relationship with God

The LORD our God, the LORD is one. Love the LORD your God with all your heart and with all your soul and with all your strength. Deuteronomy 6:4-5

Think about your friends. You visit each other often, right? You know that any relationship where you don't make an effort to spend time together and get to know each other will more than likely not survive.

The same is true of your relationship with God. You can't tell God that you love Him and not spend time in His presence. You can't say that you love Him and never read your Bible. You can't proclaim you love Him and never go to church.

You must spend time with God, whether it's in church or alone at home. We must become quiet at His feet, and get to know Him through His Word. As with any human relationship, your relationship with God will only grow if you get to know Him and spend time with Him.

The Year That Has Passed

LORD, You alone are my portion and my cup; You make my lot secure. You make known to me the path of life; You will fill me with joy in Your presence, with eternal pleasures at Your right hand. Psalm 16:5, 11

The year is almost over and for many people this is a time of reflection. Only you know about everything that has happened during the year. You know how you reacted in certain situations, and how you feel about this deep in your heart. Only you know how you've treated people and if you've improved or impoverished lives. The question you need to ask is if you think God is satisfied with the way you have lived this past year. Would He be proud if everything was made public, or would you lower your head in shame?

It's never too late to change. A new year means new beginnings to many people. Examine your heart and see where you need to start over. Should you work on your relationship with God or people? Do you need to change your attitude? Whatever it is, ask God to show you how to live for His glory in the new year.

A New Year

The LORD watches over you – the LORD is your shade at your right hand. The LORD will keep you from all harm – He will watch over your life; the LORD will watch over your coming and going both now and forevermore. Psalm 121:5, 7-8

We stand on the brink of a new year, a year full of challenges and opportunities.

Nobody knows what the future holds. For some it might be sorrow, for others unprecedented joy. For some it may mean the end of their financial struggles, and for others the solution will not yet be in sight. Many people will welcome new lives; others will lose loved ones. We just don't know what awaits us.

We can, however, be sure of one thing – that God will be with us. He will protect us from danger and keep us safe, now and forevermore. Whether the new year brings joy or sorrow, God will be with you. Never let go of His hand, stay close to Him and know He is God. He will never leave you nor forsake you.